Dump Your Stress in the Compost Pile!

DOUGLAS SCHAR

Dump Your STRESS *In The Compost Pile!*

STRESS REDUCTION THROUGH GARDENING

ELLIOTT & CLARK PUBLISHING
WASHINGTON, D.C.

To my father who taught me how to work and how to dream;
to Martha for all of her help and love; and to Kate Caldwell
for endless hours of assistance and inspiration.

Designed by Gibson Parsons Design
Edited by Elizabeth Brown Lockman
Illustrations by Charles Peale

Printed and bound in U.S.A. by Bang Printers.

Any inquiries should be directed to Elliott & Clark Publishing, P.O. Box 21038,
Washington, DC 20009-0538, telephone (202) 387-9805.

Library of Congress Cataloguing-in-Publication Data

Schar, Douglas. 1964-
    Dump your stress in the compost pile : stress reduction through
gardening / Douglas Schar.
        p.   cm.
    ISBN 1-880216-21-3 : $12.95
    1. Gardening—Therapeutic use. 2. Stress management. I. Title.
RM735.7.G37S37   1994
635'.01'9—dc20   94-4151
                                                       CIP

The author has based the material in this book on reliable historical
and scientific sources as well as upon his own personal experiences.
Every effort has been made to note potentially dangerous herbs and
potencies. The author, however, makes no guarantees as to the cura-
tive effect of any herb or tonic in this book, and no reader should
attempt to use any of the information herein provided as treatment
for any illness, weakness, or disease without first consulting a physician. Pregnant women should always consult first with a health-care
professional before taking any treatment.

CONTENTS

o you ever come home from work and sit in your car an extra few minutes to avoid speaking to your neighbor? Treat a telemarketer like dirt because he makes the mistake of invading your space just as you walk in the door? Kick an appliance because it refuses to perform its function? If any of this sounds familiar, I have some really bad news for you. You suffer from stress.

Don't even try to feel unique. An alarming number of us feel that if one more thing happens, the camel's back will break, and we will go 'round the bend. Of course, there aren't any camels or bends involved. What we are really saying is that we are handling as much as we can and any more will be too much. We are strained to the limit.

Stress is so much a fact of modern life that we tend to think it was created in the last generation, but this isn't the case at all. According to many scientists who study the problem, people have always suffered from stress. Our grandparents had just as much stress in their lives as we do. Their stress may have come from different sources, but it came in approximately the same size loads.

Surprisingly, stress is nothing new. But today's stress situation is different from that of previous generations in one important way. People in our grandparents' day didn't suffer, and I do mean suffer, from their stress as we suffer from ours. They had stress, but they knew how to get rid of it.

Stress scientists feel that the problem today is not so much our stress level as it is our lack of stress-removing activities. The older generations unloaded their stress on a daily basis. Ours sticks to us like glue. The title of this book is *Dump Your Stress in the Compost Pile!*, and it was designed by yours truly, an ex-stress-sufferer, as a guide to reduce stress through gardening. I wish I could take credit for creating all the activities in this book, but I can't. Most of them have been borrowed from earlier generations. If you continue reading, you will discover tried-and-true methods to get rid of your stress, too.

Doing so could be a matter of life or death. We all know what it feels like to be stressed out, but what we don't all realize is just how dangerous stress really is. I believe that the more you understand about the ways stress works on your body and your mind, the more likely you will be to do something about it. As they say in the military, know your enemy. Let me be the first to tell you, stress is your mortal enemy.

In its simplest terms, stress is an abbreviation for the word *distress*. The *Oxford American Dictionary* defines stress as "pressure, tension, strain." Think about someone straining to lift a heavy piece of furniture. He may get the job done, but in the process, he may also do himself some serious physical harm. People are under stress when their minds and bodies are forced to deal with more than they can comfortably handle.

Everyone has his or her own personal limits. I can lift a 100-pound bag of chicken feed without blinking an eye. My neighbor, on the other hand, would probably put her back out for a week lifting the same bag. Now if I had to carry a 200-pound bag, I would run into problems. On a different front, I can work ten hours a day comfortably, but if I have to work 12 hours, I am under stress. For some people, a 12-hour work day is no big deal. I cannot function without my sleep, others can. Part of the reason it is so difficult to define stress is that what is one person's stressor is another person's vacation.

Still, whatever our natural comfort zones are, most of us are pushed way past them on a regular basis, and while it may be hard to define stress, a person certainly knows when he is under a lot of it. Some stress-producing situations are obvious. But others, as we will see later, are more subtle. Many of us are so used to living with unresolved stress that we may not even realize how it affects us. Take a look at this list of symptoms from the American Institute of Stress.

SYMPTOMS OF STRESS

1. Frequent headaches, jaw clenching, or pain
2. Gritting or grinding of teeth
3. Stuttering or stammering
4. Tremors, trembling of lips or hands
5. Neck ache, back pain, muscle spasms

6. Light-headed, faintness, dizziness

7. Ringing, buzzing, or popping sounds

8. Frequent blushing, sweating

9. Cold or sweaty hands, feet

10. Dry mouth, problems swallowing

11. Frequent colds, infections, herpes sores

12. Rashes, itching, hives, "goose bumps"

13. Unexplained or frequent allergy attacks

14. Heartburn, stomachache, nausea

15. Excess belching, flatulence

16. Constipation, diarrhea, loss of control

17. Difficult breathing, frequent sighing

18. Sudden attacks of life-threatening panic

19. Chest pains, palpitations, rapid pulse

20. Frequent urination

21. Diminished sexual desire or performance

22. Excess anxiety, worry, guilt, nervousness

23. Increased anger, frustration, hostility

24. Depression, frequent or wild mood changes

25. Increased or decreased appetite

26. Insomnia, nightmares, disturbing dreams

27. Difficulty concentrating, racing thoughts

28. Trouble learning new information

29. Forgetfulness, disorganization, confusion

30. Difficulty in making decisions

31. Feeling overloaded or overwhelmed

32. Frequent crying spells or suicidal thoughts

33. Feelings of loneliness or worthlessness

34. Little interest in appearance, punctuality

35. Nervous habits, fidgeting, feet tapping

36. Increased frustration, irritability, edginess

37. Overreaction to petty annoyances

38. Increased number of minor accidents

39. Obsessive or compulsive behavior

40. Reduced work efficiency or productivity

41. Lies or excuses to cover up poor work

42. Rapid or mumbled speech

43. Excessive defensiveness or suspiciousness

44. Problems in communicating, sharing

45. Social withdrawal and isolation

46. Constant tiredness, weakness, fatigue

47. Frequent use of over-the-counter drugs

48. Weight gain or loss without diet

49. Increased smoking, alcohol or drug abuse

50. Excessive gambling or impulse buying

Did you find that you have more than a few of these symptoms? If so, this wouldn't be uncommon. We moderns are a people besieged by unrelieved stress. In fact, a number of experts believe that it is the underlying root of many of our social, emotional, and physical problems.

Scientists tell us that there are two kinds of stress, physical and psychological, and that both kinds affect us adversely on a daily basis. Most of us are aware of psychological stressors, but we are less attuned to the many outside influences that tax our physical bodies, making them work harder than they might otherwise have to do. One of the most basic sources of physical stress is the weather. Cold weather forces the body to expend energy to stay warm, and hot weather forces it to strive to stay cool. Dry weather draws away moisture which must be replaced.

Environmental pollution also takes its toll. If you breathe in car exhaust, for example, the chemicals in the exhaust end up in your lungs, and your body has to expend energy dealing with a problem it wasn't designed to handle. Since most of us live in polluted environments where our intake of toxins is constant, our bodies must constantly work to get rid of them, and this kind of stress is nonstop.

When you smoke cigarettes, eat food laced with artificial preservatives and flavorings, drink alcohol, or take drugs, legal or illegal, you are likewise putting chemicals into your body which it then has to cope with. The organ in charge of cleansing such toxins out of the blood is the liver. As alcohol isn't a natural part of the human diet, having to remove it strains the liver. Artificial flavorings, colorings, preservatives, and the contents of cigarette smoke likewise overburden the liver.

It's not as if your body didn't have anything else to do other than deal with such self-pollution. For one thing, the world is filled with bacteria, and this bacteria is always on the lookout to take up housekeeping inside you. Living in apartment houses, traveling on public transportation, and working in office complexes, we are exposed to many more harmful bacteria than we would be, say, on a farm. Most of us live in situations where our immune systems have to work hard all the time to keep us healthy. Think of a security guard who has to watch a building for 72 hours. Toward the end of his shift, he is tired and sloppy. He's strained the same way our immune system is strained when it's constantly bombarded with bacteria.

I hate to spring this on you, but you are an animal. Animals use their bodies to survive: birds fly around in the air, worms crawl around in the earth, and fish swim around in the water, all looking for love or a meal. Human beings were built for the same active lifestyle. Many of us spend our days sitting behind desks, pushing at little keys, and talking on the phone. Strange as it may seem, physical inactivity is a source of stress. The human body was meant to move, and not doing so represents a strain.

Our bodies were also meant to rest. Nighttime is down time for most creatures. When the sun sets, their pace slows. When was the last time you saw a bird searching for a seed at 10 P.M.? Rest is something all animals need to remain healthy. If you find yourself working when the moon is up, you are probably straining your body.

Your body is stressed, or overworked physically, on a daily basis by the very nature of modern life. But these physical stresses are only half of the equation that makes up your overall stress package. There's also psychological stress.

Psychological stress is a subjective affair. For some people, a trip to the dentist is stressful, and for others, it's no big deal. The birth of a third child may be one mother's dream come true and another's worst nightmare. Events in life affect each of us differently, but for all of us, the major source of psychological stress is change.

When things change in your life, you are required to process a lot of new information as you find ways to cope with your new situation. Learning requires energy, and this strains the mind and the body. Not much stays the same for long in the modern world, and this means that most of us are subject to a nonstop bombardment of stress.

Some scientists got together a number of years ago and compiled a list of life changes that result in stress. It's called the "Social Readjustment Rating Scale," and it's worth taking a look.

SOCIAL READJUSTMENT RATING SCALE

RANK	LIFE EVENT	MEAN VALUE
1	Death of a spouse	100
2	Divorce	73
3	Marital separation	65
4	Jail term	63
5	Death of a close family member	63
6	Personal injury or illness	53
7	Marriage	50
8	Fired at work	47
9	Marital reconciliation	45
10	Retirement	45
11	Change in health of family member	44
12	Pregnancy	40
13	Sex difficulties	39
14	Gain of new family member	39
15	Business adjustment	39
16	Change in financial state	38
17	Death of a close friend	37
18	Change to different line of work	36
19	Change in number of arguments with spouse	35
20	Mortgage over $10,000 (in 1967)	31
21	Foreclosure of mortgage or loan	30
22	Change in responsibilities at work	29

Reprinted with permission from J. Psychosomat. Res., 11:213:218, 1967, Holmes, T. H. and Rahe, R. H., The Social Readjustment Scale. Copyright, Pergamon Press., Ltd.

You may have noticed that these life changes are ranked according to the level of stress produced and that each life change is given a point value. The idea is to read through the list, figure out how many of the changes apply to you, and add up the number of stress points you have. Go ahead and see how you do.

With this figure in mind, be prepared for another bit of bad news. The scientists who put the list together also found that persons with scores of 200 or more were almost assured of developing a serious illness. Contrary to Western medicine's traditional notion that the mind and body are separate entities with little or no interconnection, stress scientists tell us that psychological stress affects us physically.

The American Institute of Stress has this to say:

The important role of stress in health and illness has been increasingly confirmed by recent scientific research. Various surveys report that 75 to 90 percent of all visits to primary care physicians are for stress related complaints. These include headache, backache, insomnia, anxiety, depression, arthritis, herpes, gastrointestinal and skin problems, obesity, alcoholism, and drug abuse complications. Stress also plays a prominent role in heart attacks, hypertension, cancer, and the aging process. It is generally not appreciated that stress has a much more profound effect on cholesterol levels than diet.

According to the director of the institute, Dr. Paul J. Rosch, stress is "taking a terrible toll on the nation's health and economy. It is a heavy contributor to heart disease, cancer, respiratory distress, lupus, and many other life-threatening illnesses. It is a key reason for our astronomic health care costs." The stress doctor goes on to say that every week 12 million people take medication for stress-related symptoms and that it costs American business $150 billion each year in absenteeism, lost productivity, accidents, and medical insurance.

Let's take this stress-and-the-body talk from the general to the specific. Heart disease is one of the leading causes of death in America today. Most American men (and an increasing number of women) will die from it. The following coronary killers are all said to be directly related to unrelieved stress: angina pectoris, atherosclerosis (fatty infiltration of the arteries), arteriosclerosis (calcification or hardening of the arteries), cardiac arrhythmias (abnormal heart rhythm), coronary artery disease (coronary thrombosis, myocardial infarction, heart attack), congestive heart failure, and cerebral stroke. If you're a man, you are likely to die clutching your chest. Even if you don't die of heart disease, most of the men you know will.

This was not true a century ago. Heart disease is a relatively new killer, and the scary fact is that there has been a direct relationship between America's increase in gross national product and the percentage of American deaths due to heart disease. Americans have the highest rate of heart disease in the world. Until recently everybody placed the blame on our typically high-cholesterol diet, but stress researchers now feel that this may be entirely off the mark. If you thought you had eliminated the possibility of heart disease by trading in your morning bacon for granola, not so fast.

Since the 1960s, there has been a total turnaround in Americans' awareness of high-cholesterol foods. Our diets are lower in fat today than they were 40 years ago, but our heart disease rate has increased and continues to increase every year. Correcting our diets has not corrected our heart disease problems.

Increasingly, stress looks like the prime suspect. In a study made in the late 1940s, heart doctors found that of men and women eating the same diet, namely husbands and wives, the men had the heart disease and the women didn't. At that time, the wives worked at home, and the husbands worked in offices. As these people took all their meals together, the difference in their stress loads seemed to account for the difference in their health.

Another study done at the same time found that Mexican and African American women did tend to suffer from heart disease. Unlike their white contemporaries, a large percentage of these women were in the labor force due to socioeconomic factors. The price of getting to run in the rat race was the same for these women as it was for the white men: death by heart failure. Researchers in a more recent study determined that 90 percent of heart patients had a high level of stress in their lives.

Are you sick yet? I haven't finished. A group of accountants were

The modern world gives us a hundred different sources of stress and few good ways to relieve it.

studied during their two most stressful periods, the end of the tax year and the end of the fiscal year. Surprise, surprise, the entire group, regardless of dietary differences, experienced a peak in their cholesterol level during these times. It seems that a high cholesterol level, the cause of much heart disease, is directly linked to stress. Stress causes elevated cholesterol!

Researchers feel that beyond suffering from high cholesterol, people under a lot of pressure simply wear their cardiovascular systems out. Every deadline, every mad rush to the office, every frantic night of late work, raises the blood pressure and puts a strain on the body. Typically, as our pace of life has increased, our down time has decreased. We sleep less, relax less, and vacation less. We have less time to dump our stress. On top of overusing the arterial system on a daily basis, we don't rest that system properly. All of this combines to produce an unhappy result for you and your kin: you drop dead at age 55.

Stress doesn't limit itself to the circulatory system. It wears out all parts of the body, tearing them down so that they can't do their jobs. Perhaps the scariest function stress erodes is that of the immune system, which helps keep dangerous bacteria out of the body and cancerous cells under control.

Not to make you paranoid, but as you read this, there are several million pathogenic bacteria and virus swarming around your body, fighting their way to get in. Most are killed by the immune system at the point

Stress kills—unless you've made alternative plans.

of entry, the nose and the mouth. But get yourself under some stress—your daughter gets married, your boss gives you a big assignment, your husband leaves you—and boom, you get a cold. It's commonly understood that periods of high stress often end with some kind of infection.

How does stress undermine your body's ability to stay well? Let's start with a little anatomy lesson. Basically, your body is sealed tight to bacteria. If you get something in your eye, the brain tells the eye to water and get whatever the heck it is out and fast. If you cut yourself, the area swells up with white blood cells, sealing the wound off to the rest of the body. Your immunity system creates a barrier between your innards and the outside world.

Have you ever noticed that when you start to feel a cold setting in, your glands swell? That's because they are working overtime to produce lymphocytes, the bacteria-killing cells needed to fight whatever has made its way into your body. These lymphocytes have the ability to distinguish between good bacteria and bad. They are also in charge of killing cancer clusters in the bud. The good they let pass, the bad cells they hit with their handy laser guns.

This system was built to work, so it does. That is, until you add some stress to the equation. When the mind and body are subject to stress, the immunity system slows down and bacteria have an opportunity to get past the guards.

Here's what happens. Your emotional upset sends a wake-up call to your hypothalamus gland. This sends a signal to your pituitary gland, and the pituitary gland notifies the adrenal cortex gland that a little adrenalin is needed. Aside from adrenalin, the adrenal cortex gland, your "fight or flight" gear box, also produces a nasty substance called glucocorticoid which gets pumped out and shipped to the entire body when you're under stress. What does this mean? In a nutshell, the immune system doesn't function as well as it does under normal circumstances. A properly functioning body takes care of cancer cells along with bacteria before they get out of control. Stress causes cancer by knocking out the first line of defense, internal policing.

In case you need more convincing, let me tell you a little bit about cholera. In days gone by, before its near eradication, this deadly disease struck in epidemic fashion. Interestingly enough, though, it tended to kill more adults than children.

With cholera, the terminal trouble starts when bacteria passes from the stomach into the intestinal tract. Fortunately, this usually doesn't occur because there are a lot of bacteria-killing roadblocks between those two points. However, if someone is nervous, the resulting change in stomach acidity allows the cholera bacteria to reach the intestines. Children don't worry about epidemics; parents do. Guess who usually died from cholera? The mommies and daddies. Cholera killed them because they suffered from the stress of being grownups.

We've only looked at the circulatory and immunity systems, but believe me when I say that stress damages every system you possess. I have the studies sitting in front of me to prove it. If you don't do something to get rid of stress, it will get rid of you.

To make matters a little more personal, I suggest that you take an inventory of the stresses in your life. Draw a line down the middle of a piece of paper. On the left half, write the physical stressors in your life, and on the right half, write the psychological stressors. Put down at least, and I mean at least, ten of each kind. Now make a list of all the stress-related illnesses from which you suffer. Stress attacks each person differently: some people get stomachaches, others rashes. Take some time to think about what happens to your body when you're under stress and write your findings on the back of your stress inventory. The better you catalogue the stress in your life, the better you will be able to dump it.

THE SOLUTION

Stress is an inescapable fact of life. But holding onto it and keeping it around like a pet dog is up to you. If you want to get rid of your stress, you can. If you want to live to a ripe old age, you need to practice stress management.

For starters, in both the physical and the psychological categories, there are two kinds of stress: obligatory and optional. Some stressors you can't do anything about and others you can. The first step in a stress-management program is establishing what stress falls into what category. The key here is to ditch the optional stress wherever possible. If you live in a polluted city, there isn't much you can do about the dirty air you breathe. On the other hand,

Taking a tiptoe through the tulips is the stress sufferer's best resort.

you can choose what you eat, and you might want to avoid foods packed with artificial colorings, flavorings, and preservatives. Give up diet sodas and pick up apple cider.

As for psychological stressors, you have no choice but to deal with a relative's death, but overcommitting yourself to nonessential activities is your decision. You may have to look for a new job if you get laid off; you don't have to coach the Little League team at the same time. Go back to your inventory, circle the sources of stress that you have chosen, and choose to get rid of them. Eliminate as much physical and psychological stress as you possibly can.

After that's done, you'll still have plenty of stress on your list and in your life. Never fear, there are ways to reduce its toxic effects. You can quite literally dump your stress in the compost pile. How can a person do this? Read on.

As we all know, stress exhausts people, depleting them of vital strength and energy. In response to this exhaustion, folks drink tremendous amounts of caffeine and take huge numbers of amphetamines every year. While we all need energy to get through the day, we don't need the kind of energy that further stresses our bodies, and that's just what caffeine and amphetamines do.

At the end of a stressful day, most people feel the need to unwind. Many of us do this by cracking open a beer or swallowing a tranquilizer. Using these substances may make us feel a little better in the short run, but it is only a

Band-Aid over a problem that will not go away. In fact, using substances to relax only adds to the physical stress we are already under.

What we really need is to dump our stress and receive an infusion of energy. Now here's the shocker: by gardening you can do both. I know it doesn't make sense. How can adding one more activity to an already over-booked day do anything but acerbate the problem? I know it is a paradox, but gardening removes tension and replaces it with serenity and power.

Luther Burbank was a famous American gardener who fled the East Coast at the end of the 19th century and moved to California. Once there he opened a nursery where he practiced his specialty, creating new plant varieties out of old ones. Many plant breeders would settle for introducing one new variety. Burbank introduced thousands upon thousands. What's more, the man worked night and day without strain.

Burbank credited his tremendous energy to having an active association with nature. He felt that if you connected yourself with nature, it would pro-vide you with all the vitality you could ever need. He said that gardening would give a person a peaceful mind and a powerful body. It's my personal belief that the reason folks in days gone by were able to handle the stress in their lives better than we handle ours is that they had a direct relationship with nature. As Luther Burbank would say, they were connected to the power source.

The idea of losing your stress through nature and replacing it with peaceful energy may sound a little shaky, but chances are you already know that it works. Think about a trip to the beach. After a tough period on the job, you take off and head for the ocean. You spend a week walking in the sand, floating in the sea, tasting the salty brine, feeling the sun on your back and the sand between your fingers. The first couple of days you are still edgy; by the end of the week, you're as loose as ashes. You go back to work after this nature treatment, and the biggest jerk in the office feels like a friend. The traffic snarl doesn't bother you much, and you're actually pleasant to the telemarketer who rings your home at the dinner hour.

Scientific studies have demonstrated that when folks under stress were shown a series of natural scenes, they experienced a reduction in respiration rate and cardiovascular pressure. Merely seeing the images of plants, trees, and birds calmed their bodies and raised their spirits. Don't you love it when science proves stuff you already knew? A walk through a quiet forest is going to make a person feel better than a walk down a major highway.

The healing that takes place when we connect ourselves with nature is real. Unfortunately, many of us don't live by the ocean. We live in the suburbs and get to the mountains or sea once a year if we're lucky. The big secret is that gardening in your own backyard can afford you the same peaceful, powerful feeling you get walking on the beach, hiking in the mountains, or canoeing on a river. The best news is that you don't have to wait all year long for your vacation to do it. You can step out your back door into your garden and get that same feeling on a daily basis.

A group of scientists is looking into what is dubbed "human well-being and horticulture." Studying the impact that gardening has on the body and mind, these researchers have found that people who garden live longer than people who don't. Gardening also makes people feel better and improves their health, both mental and physical. The power of gardening is so absolute that gardening is used as a tool of rehabilitation for prison inmates, emotionally disturbed children, and the mentally ill in programs across the country. The results of these programs have all been the same: folks get better when they get involved with a garden.

I will take this moment to offer my own personal testimony. I was once a person who suffered from stress, mentally, physically, and spiritually. I had always had a garden as a child, but when I went off to college in New York City, my gardening went by the wayside. Eventually I graduated and came back home. I had an adult life and adult stress, and I started gardening again. To my surprise, I discovered that no matter how tough my day had been, a few minutes of weeding and fussing in my garden resulted in a clear-cut change in my mood and attitude. The stress was swept away and replaced by something infinitely better—peace of mind.

Gardening is an experiential thing: the more you do it, the more you know. I have spent the past seven years refining my own personal gardening therapy. I have taught these techniques to a number of folks, and the experience they have had parallels mine: gardening makes them feel better. If you follow the instructions in this book, install one or more of the stress-relieving theme gardens, and do the exercises I've included, I guarantee that you will feel better, too.

LESSON NUMBER ONE

Most of us have been thoroughly schooled in the fine art of stressing ourselves out. We are the masters of rush. We overcommit, and we don't take care of ourselves. If we want to deal with our stress problem, we are going to have to learn to do things differently.

It's a foregone conclusion that the average day is filled with stress, and that by the end of it, we are bushed. Now, what do most of us do as soon as we get home? We grab our mail, pick up the messages on the answering machine, and turn on the evening news.

Think about what this does to you. Remember, the day is over, and you are already stressed out. The first thing you do in this exhausted state is collect your mail. Perhaps your mail is different than my mail, but mine is all bills—folks just don't write like they used to. Earlier we learned that when stressed-out people were presented with scenes of nature, they experienced a drop in blood pressure and an improved mental outlook. Somehow, I think, and it's just a hunch, that the same people, if presented with a stack of bills, would experience a rise in blood pressure. Suffice it to say that reviewing one's accounts is not what a person operating on negative energy needs to do at the end of the workday.

After the mail, we head for

Stress may be hard to describe, but we all know what too much of it feels like.

22

the answering machine, which invariably has messages on it. At a bare minimum, these messages will be from people demanding a return phone call, and usually a whole lot more. Next, we turn on the TV to see whatever human tragedy the media has tracked down for the day.

What's wrong with this picture? You come home from your day all stressed out, and what do you do? Sign up for a little bit more.

Here is the first change you must make if you are serious about getting rid of your stress problem. Rather than hitting the mailbox first, head to the garden. I mean walk from the car, bus, or subway, and proceed directly to the garden. Let the bills stay in the box. They won't go anywhere, and the messages on the machine won't evaporate. Let the announcements of the day's horror remain somebody else's problem. Retrain yourself to head to the garden as soon as you get home, even if there's nothing planted in it yet.

Of course, it would be helpful if there was something out there for you to look at. But before we get to the one-two-three's of setting up a stress-relieving garden, we need to talk about what it is we are trying to create. We are trying to create a garden. We are not trying to create a yard.

In my mind, yards are for neighbors, and gardens are for the people who own the house. The next time you see someone in your neighborhood installing a bunch of new plants, notice how she goes out to the street and takes a gander at the placement of a tree before digging the hole for it. When you think about how plants will appear to people on the outside looking in, you are working on a yard.

Let's get clear on one thing right now: this book is not about planning a yard. It's about planning a garden. A garden is a place for you to be and to enjoy. It's a place for you to hide from the world and the pressures it creates, not a perfect picture for the neighbors. The vantage point to check the placement of your tree is not from the street, but rather from inside the garden. No one else has to like your garden; no one else has to come into it. I know it sounds like semantics, but this is a critical point.

The idea is to create an oasis for yourself. You probably haven't given the idea of oasis much thought, but I have. While traveling in the Middle East a few years ago, I had the chance to experience an oasis firsthand, and it had a profound effect on my ideas about gardens.

I was driving through the desert in a little car packed with people, minus the comfort of air-conditioning. The car was hot, I was hot, everything was hot. The black highway provided the only color in the drab landscape—beige, beige, and more beige. The strangest part of the experience was the wind. Most winds I've experienced are cool, but not this one. The sensation was like standing in front of a house-sized blow dryer set on high.

I remember being conscious of two things. The first was that no matter how much water I drank, I could not quench my thirst. The second was a sensation: I felt as if I was covered with a coat of chalk dust. At a certain point, the monotony of the landscape just about made me nuts. Everything the other passengers had to say became annoying, and all I could think was, "Will this trip ever end?"

We finally spotted a tiny blip of green on the horizon. The green blip grew as we got closer and became a big stand of trees encircling a lake. Maybe it was really a pond, but in my state of mind, it looked like a lake. My fellow passengers informed me that this greenness was an oasis and that we could stop and take a rest. At that moment, I knew there was a God.

Your garden should be a private oasis, a place removed from all the madness of contemporary life.

24

When we arrived at the oasis, my companions and I splashed in the water and wandered among all the plants. Some were in bloom and others loaded with fruits. After an hour of frolicking in the green, we jumped back in the car, refreshed and happy to drive on. The break made it possible to deal with more of the tiresome landscape and uncomfortable journey.

As far as I'm concerned, the modern world is a desert for the human spirit. We all need a refuge from traffic, bosses, political disasters, and the phone, a place to escape the pressures and stresses of our daily lives. I suggest that you develop your garden into a little oasis.

"PRIVATIZING" YOUR GARDEN

The other day I was having brunch at a friend's house, and I heard a wild woman on a real tirade about her officemates. Several of them were constantly on her about the fact that she lived in the city. They were suburbanites, and they were always telling her how they couldn't give up all their exterior space for the typically tiny lots city dwellers have. The woman pointed out something to the people at the brunch, and apparently to her coworkers, too. What she said was this: "If people in the suburbs so desperately need all that wonderful outdoor space, how come you never see them in it? You can drive from suburb to suburb on a Saturday or Sunday and see nary a soul outside."

This is true. People in the city do tend to use their exterior space more than people in the suburbs. Few of my suburban friends spend their leisure time in the garden, whereas all of my city friends use what outdoor areas they have all season long—barbecuing, gardening, laying out, and doing whatever else comes to mind. I believe that this is the case for one simple reason: privacy.

Suburban yards tend to be open front and back. In the front yard, you have all the people driving by, and in the backyard, you have all the other neighbors looking out their windows. In the city, backyards are usually fenced and private. Though they are much smaller and in even closer proximity to the neighbors than suburban yards, they often give a very secure and secluded feeling. Between the fences and hedges, you can't see your neighbors, and they can't see you. This may be an illusion, but it works.

I think that folks with open yards don't go into them very often because

While decreasing your personal stress load, your garden may increase that of your neighbors. Oh, well, nothing's perfect!

they don't feel safe there. They feel exposed, and this is the last thing a stressed-out person needs. Most days after work, would you want to run out to the garden if the entire world was going to watch you do it? Chances are the answer to this question is no, and for this reason, the first step in creating your oasis is to make it private. Start thinking about how you can convert your outdoor area from an exposed to an intimate, safe-feeling space. If yours is already like this, terrific. You will probably want to go ahead and read on anyway to pick up some tips on how to make a good thing even better.

Think of your garden oasis in terms of a room. Most rooms have walls, and our first job is to create the walls that will, in turn, create the room. Typically, we have only to think about three of the four walls, as the house creates the first barrier between the backyard and the outside world.

The word *barrier* is important here. One of the hallmarks of a well "privatized" garden, and consequently of one that feels safe and comfortable, is that the space is clearly defined. When you are in the garden, it should be obvious that's where you are, and when you are standing outside of the garden, it should be equally obvious. This is not the case with most suburban yards.

In our somewhat democratic nation, there is a great deal of hesitancy to plainly and boldly declare, "This yard is mine, and I will do with it what I wish." Apparently the notion of lawns, one bleeding into the next with no visual breaks, was a major part of the original design for suburbs. Rather than compete to have the most inventive and individual garden, everyone in the suburbs tries to make his yard just as mediocre as the one on either side.

"Privatizing" your garden may go against the unwritten rule: "Thou shalt not do whatever thou wants with thine yard." For one reason or another, neighbors tend to feel proprietary about your land as well as their own, and they can get pretty feisty when they see your project under way. Be prepared. Creating the visual walls you need to define your private space is a declaration of ownership. If your neighbors have a problem with this, just tell them that they get a vote when they start paying the mortgage on your house.

Remember, though, that the object here is not to alienate the folks next door. The object is to create a cozy, private space that is inviting to spend time in. "Cozy" and "private" are the feelings you want. Blocking is the technique you will use to bring those feelings about. You will create your second, third, and fourth walls with techniques that block out your view of your neighbors and your neighbors' view of you.

Here are some traditional and some not-so-traditional means of creating the visual walls you'll need. Review the options and see which ones appeal to you. If none of them suits your taste, figure out another way to create privacy that does. How you choose to physically define your garden space is entirely up to you.

FENCING

If you like fences and are willing to pay for one, this is a great option to explore. A big fence creates instant privacy. The mistake people make with the fence idea is not taking it far enough. A four-foot fence creates privacy for your hips and toes, and that's about it. If you're going to spend the money on fencing, think about going higher, to six feet or more. Here's the rule for putting up a fence: if you can still see your neighbors seeing you, you haven't gone high enough.

Obviously an eight-foot fence is more expensive than a six-foot fence. But there is a way to extend the six-foot fence that is both simple and relatively inexpensive. When you build the fence or have it built, replace every other fence post with an eight-foot post. Then, starting above six feet, run heavy cable wire at three equal intervals moving up the length of the rod. These

Don't be shy when it comes to "privatizing" your space. Remember, this is a matter of life or death, and the death that we're talking about is yours!

wires will create an arbor. Plant and train vines on them, and in a matter of two years, you'll have an eight-foot privacy fence. You will have traditional fencing for the bottom six feet and green fencing for the top two.

The combination can be much more lovely than a plain fence. Grapes are a natural choice for the arbor, but kiwis, wisteria, trumpet vine, and hops are also great plants to use.

You can extend this idea a little further by skipping the fence part altogether and settling for a simple trellis covered with vines. Just put in eight-foot rods, string the wire from top to bottom at equal intervals, and plant one or several types of vines on the wire. This way you can create an eight-foot privacy fence for the cost of the poles and wire and a few vines. The object here is to create a visual separation, not necessarily a physical one. A green arbor that blocks your view does the job just fine and can be much less expensive than the true physical barrier.

If you are thinking right now that there is no way you want to fence in your property, hold your horses. In my years as a landscape designer, I found that many people are repulsed by the idea of fencing. This is largely because they have only experienced fencing poorly done. By this I don't mean fencing poorly constructed, I mean fencing poorly done. Leaving a fence bare is about as appealing as leaving the walls of a new house unpainted sheetrock. Proper treatment of the fence after it has been built makes all the difference.

You see, the problem really isn't the fence. The problem is what you do with the fence. Fences need to be softened with plant materials. Once built, you need to cover it with vines and obscure it with trees and bushes. Accessorize, accessorize! If you treat your fence properly, you will be well on your way to developing your own personal Garden of Eden.

PLANTINGS

If you still don't like the idea of fencing your garden, don't despair. There's another option to accomplish the same thing: *hedges*. Hedges are one of God's greatest gifts to the gardener. They're inexpensive and easy to install, and while they may take a little time to accomplish their mission, accomplish it they will. As an example, privet hedge can grow two feet a year—in three years, you will have a six-foot visual barrier. Privet is fast growing, cheap, and hard to kill. One of the oldest hedge materials around, its name is a bastardization of *prive*, the French word for "private."

Of course, a plain old privet hedge can lend a certain San Quentin feeling to a space; as with fences, such hedges require a little softening. A few trees inserted just behind the row of hedges and a few groupings of other shrubs to the front will do wonders. You might want to add some blooming trees—cherry, crabapple, or magnolia—to interrupt the green expanse of privet.

Actually, the most attractive way to create a visual barrier for your garden may be to use a combination of techniques. A little fencing here and little hedging there add up to the most textural and rich privacy design.

Armed with some blocking options, go to work on your own space. Somewhere in your files there is a copy of your plat. Take it to the photocopying shop and make yourself some copies you can scribble on. Look at the perimeters of your proposed gardening area and sketch in some possible barriers,

imagining what they would look like. Then draw some more. Tinker around until you come up with something that you like. Remember, your object is to create a private space to garden in, a place within which you can feel alone and secure, a place where you can dump your stress and commune with the original power source. Once you have a blocking plan in mind, set about getting it installed. I think you will discover that as soon as your garden is "privatized," it will become warm and welcoming. Suddenly you will feel drawn out into the garden.

Your garden should be so private that you don't even know your neighbors exist.

WHAT TO GROW IN YOUR GARDEN

Lawns are filled with obligatory plants: a few shrubs along the foundation of the house, maybe a tree in the middle of the yard, and a boatload of grass in between. A garden is filled with plants that thrill and exhilarate the gardener.

Many people have told me that they are not interested in gardening. You yourself may have had the same thought. In my experience, people who feel this way usually have lawns filled with the most lackluster plants in the history of the universe. Take the yew as an example. Almost every yard in America has a few yews in it, and it's hard to think of a more boring bush. It's green year-round, and its only noteworthy feature is those red, mushy, and highly poisonous berries that splatter the walkway once a year. What's to get excited about?

If you think gardening doesn't interest you, it's only because you haven't explored all the options out there. There's something for everyone in the world of gardening, and your next assignment is to discover which plants and gardening techniques will really give you a kick. If after a little research, you still can't find something that excites you, you probably are already dead and don't need a garden to relieve your stress any more.

In working out a stress-management plan, you have to get tricky with yourself. You can lose your stress by spending half an hour in the garden every day, but that's assuming that you actually go out there and spend the time. Rather than heaping one more disciplined, scheduled activity into your life, trick yourself into complying with the program. How does a person do this? Fill the garden with plants that thrill you, and you will run outside as soon as you get home because you are so excited to see what has happened with them while you were away. Don't discipline, inspire. Replace that boring yew with a plant that appeals to you, and you won't have to remind yourself to go to the garden. You will gravitate there naturally.

The key is planting plants that you really like, plants that amuse or delight. For example, one of the most exciting plants I grow is the watermelon. When I plant five or six watermelon seeds, a vine explodes out of the ground almost immediately. In a few weeks' time, I spot lemon-sized watermelons, and with each week that passes, these baby watermelons just get bigger and bigger. Before long, they have developed into 30-pound fruits.

During the summer, I often go to the watermelon patch just to see how much the melons have grown that day. When the fruit is ripe, I run out with a knife, cut a melon from the vine, and sit in my garden chair, eating away.

Now this is a subjective thing. I like eating watermelon. If you hate watermelon, you probably wouldn't run out to the garden, filled with glee and anticipation as one of the melons ripens. Growing watermelon would be a bad choice for you. I promise you this, though. If your garden contains plants that don't make your heart

One of the best parts of the process is discovering which plants will give you maximum joy. Seek and you shall find.

go pitter-patter, you won't find yourself there very often. I've included seven quite different theme gardens in this book because I wanted to offer you some options.

What kind of plants would thrill you? Flowers to cut for the house or to leave right where they are for a lift after a long day at the office? Vegetables for dinner, fruit for Sunday breakfast, herbs for their flavoring or health-giving powers? If you've gardened before, you might already have a handle on this. If you haven't, it's time to do some exploration. It's time to see what plants make you happy!

This discovery process is so important that I am going to ask you to put down this book, pack yourself into your car, and head either to the library or to an upscale bookseller. Spend an hour or so leafing through illustrated gardening books and magazines. Your mission is to discover pictures that really excite you. Look at English gardening books, Japanese gardening books, flower gardening books, herb gardening books, vegetable gardening books—whatever. Keep looking until you have found some area in the plant kingdom that attracts you. Maybe it's roses; maybe it's bushes trimmed in the shapes of barnyard animals.

You might also want to look at a few mail-order nursery catalogues. There are hundreds of companies that sell plant materials through the mail, and their catalogues are just packed with plant options and lovely color pictures thereof. Getting your hands on some of these is a fabulous way to discover what you'd like for your garden without even leaving the house.

It's also the ideal way to shop once you know what you want. Not only is picking up the phone or dropping an envelope in the mailbox easier than driving to a gardening center, it's usually cheaper. As mail-order places don't have the overhead of stores, they tend to offer better prices. They're definitely a boon to stress-sufferers. Here are the names and addresses of some old favorites. More are included at the ends of each chapter.

J. W. JUNG SEED COMPANY
335 S. High Street
Randolph, WI 53957-0001
800-247-JUNG

PARK SEED COMPANY
Cokesbury Road
Greenwood, SC 29647-0001
803-223-7333

W. ATLEE BURPEE COMPANY   GURNEY'S SEED & NURSERY COMPANY

300 Park Avenue   110 Capital Street

Warminster, PA 18974   Yankton, SD 57079

800-888-1447   605-665-1671

Write down the names of all the plants you'd like to grow. Then, when it comes time to make your garden, you'll have your shopping list ready. Don't worry whether the plants you have amassed make sense together. They don't have to. This garden is for you, and as long as it is filled with plants that you are excited about, it will be a success.

This is how my present stress-relieving garden developed. Before moving to Washington, D.C., I lived in Manhattan for some years, and while I had managed to do some gardening on the terrace of my Soho loft and in the tiny front yard of my Gramercy Park flat, I was seriously limited by the obvious space constraints. When I moved to D.C., I bought a place in a residential part of the city. I had a standard city yard, 50 feet wide and 80 feet deep, with a huge piece in the middle taken out by the house.

I moved in the summer, and as soon as I got settled, I sent away for every mail-order gardening catalogue known to man. By October, they started arriving. Being a disorganized and emotional shopper by nature, I ordered a little of this and that from just about every company. After gardening on a fire escape, I was a bit overzealous and bought anything that appealed to me. What's more, I didn't keep track of what I had ordered. The net result was that the following spring enough plant materials to cover a ten-acre farm arrived and had to be fit into my tiny city lot.

Somehow I managed, and in short order my yard became a garden, a wonderland filled with the strange and the common, each plant more captivating than the next. Take a lesson from my experience. As you contemplate filling up your garden, don't worry so much about details. Concern yourself with growing the plants that you love, and the rest will take care of itself.

If you notice a flower in a neighbor's yard that appeals to you, ask for a cutting and stick it in wherever it will fit. If you see a plant at the garden center that seems provocative, buy it. Allow yourself to be a child again. Most of us have a serious adult facade which we display to the rest of the world. To

When it comes to selecting plants for your garden, give the adult within you a day off.

create a fabulous garden, you need to drop the facade and find the whimsical, unrealistic, silly, and naive child that still exists somewhere deep inside you. Let him or her pick the plants that will grow in your garden. Your ultimate goal is to create a garden in which you can play like a child. Being an adult has its place, and it's not in the garden. After all, it was the grownups who bit the dust from cholera, not the little kids.

The following stress-relieving theme gardens are here for you to explore and learn from. If you find that you really enjoy a certain type of gardening, you may want to explore the possibilities a little more fully. By all means, jump in and learn away—the more involved you get with your garden, the more stress you are going to unload. That's why each chapter includes an informal meet-and-greet session with the suggested plants and a list of additional resources.

Don't limit yourself to books and magazines, though. The world of gardening is filled with people ready and willing to share their experience with you. Ask a neighbor how he gets his roses to bloom so spectacularly, and you will have a firsthand account of how to get roses to do the same in your own yard. Talk with the woman at the local farmer's market about how she grows such sweet tomatoes, and you'll be on your way to growing some, too. The point is to do what makes you happy, to create the kind of garden where you can best dump the stress from your life. These garden plans were created to help me relieve my own stress. My hope is that they will assist you in doing the same.

Most of us who suffer from stress tend not to really see, feel, hear, smell, or taste the world around us. Rushing here and there, we tune out and lose touch with our senses. When was the last time you actually tasted the flavors in a fresh apple? When was the last time you listened quietly to the sounds of the street or the rain? If you suffer from stress, chances are that your answer is: "Not in a long while."

A big part of stress management is slowing your pace down, if only for a few minutes a day. Nature offers you the gift of peace, but you must slow down so that she can hand it to you. Slowing down to hear, to see, to feel, to taste, or to smell slows you down to nature's pace. Now this isn't going to be easy for you, but you can do it. The "stress-ercises" included with each gardening plan are here to help you along. These sensory-awakening activities will allow you to rediscover your senses and the pleasures they can bring, and if you want to fully dump your stress in the compost pile, you had better do them! (You know what the alternative is.)

Most stress sufferers are out of touch with the wonders around them. Use your garden to rediscover senses you may have forgotten you have.

CHAPTER ONE

The Tonic Garden

As we have learned, stress has a physical as well as a psychological dimension. The Tonic Garden will help you deal with both. On the psychological side, tending the herbs in this garden will give you the contact with nature you need. On the physical side, the herbs contained in this garden plan are all tonic plants. These are plants which when taken in tea on a regular basis strengthen and reinvigorate the body. No one knows exactly how tonic plants improve the general health, but their ability to do so has been noted for centuries. They can undo the damage done by stress left undumped for too long.

The generations that came before us did a number of things to reverse the effects of stress, and one of them was taking tonics on a regular basis. Here's what a physician, R. V. Pierce, had to say about tonics in 1895:

Tonics are a class of medicines which in some inexplicable manner gradually change certain morbid actions of the system, and establish a healthy condition instead. They stimulate the vital processes to renewed activity, and arouse the excretory organs to remove matter which ought to be eliminated. They facilitate the action of the

You won't be the first person to go from a broken-down wreck to a sleek specimen of stress-free humanity with a little garden therapy.

secretory glands, tone them up, and give a new impulse to their operation, so that they can more expeditiously rid the system of worn out and effete materials. In this way they alter, correct, and purify the fluids, tone up the organs, and re-establish their healthy function.

Sounds like just what the doctor ordered! The use of tonics has fallen out of favor in recent times. Due to the current health-care crisis and the high cost of medical services, however, I believe that we soon will see their rediscovery. What was part of earlier generations' frontal assault in the war on stress is about to be called back into duty.

The herbs in our garden not only build up the overall constitution, they also treat the more immediate symptoms of stress: headache, insomnia, stomachache, nervousness, and more. Imagine running out to the garden after a tough day and gathering a handful of plants which, when tossed into a pot, covered with boiling water, and then steeped, create a tea that will make all the tension drain out of your head. When you take your tea outside and slowly sip it in the middle of your private oasis, not only does the tea immediately relax you, it also works to undo the damage the day's stress has caused. Sounds pretty great, doesn't it? Well, this can all be yours quite easily.

For one reason or another, inexperienced gardeners, who, I might add, make up the better portion of our population, believe that growing herbs is a task better left to the experts. They're wrong. Herbs are some of the easiest plants to grow. In fact, herb gardening is so easy that you might want to let your three-year-old do it.

Our most common herbs are the weeds of Europe, Asia Minor, and North Africa. There they are not cultivated; they just grow wild like dandelions and crab grass. People in Greece don't buy oregano. They go out to the side of the road and gather it. On one trip to the south of France, I was shocked to see thyme growing in an abandoned lot. Suffice it to say that this garden plan and the resulting garden will not take much time out of your already busy schedule. Essentially these weeds grow themselves.

There are two kinds of plants that a person can put into the garden, perennial and annual. Perennial plants are planted once and come back from the roots year after year. Annual plants live their entire life cycle in the space of one season and then die. The herbs contained in this garden plan are for the most part perennial, which means that they will continue to come up each spring for as long as you have the garden. This is a handy feature for the busy gardener—no yearly replanting necessary! Plant them once, and you'll have herbs for life.

DILL

Dill, or dill weed as it is commonly known, is the tension-gripped stomach's best friend. The plant's seeds and leaves contain chemicals which can settle a nervous stomach and improve digestion. For those who find themselves burping after a tough day, dill weed offers welcome relief.

The digestive tract and its importance are grossly underestimated in today's society. As the stomach is responsible for feeding the entire body, people with poor digestion can anticipate having poor bodies. Chronic stomach complaints, most of which come from unresolved stress, are a very serious problem. Folks with such problems should take it upon themselves to do whatever they can to see that their stomachs function properly; that is, if they want to stay alive for any lengthy period of time.

Dill is a member of one of the most medicinal of the plant families, the umbelifera family. This clutch of famous relations includes angelica, carrot, parsnip, parsley, fennel, anise, coriander, caraway, celery, asafoetida, and many more. All the members of this family are used around the world to improve the functioning of the digestive tract and thereby the overall health.

If you've ever ordered seeds from a catalogue, you've probably noticed that there are two kinds of cucumbers: burpless and nonburpless. I had known this for years but never really understood the difference until I took a trip to the Middle East and found out firsthand.

I was traveling with some Bedouin traders. In our little car packed with too many people was a big bag of cool cucumbers, which people in the desert often carry for refreshment. Being terribly thirsty, I ate a good half-dozen. After about an hour, I started burping, which is something I almost never do. My belly started swelling, and by the end of the trip I looked as if I was expecting twins. I burped heinously for days and became concerned that I had picked up some nasty intestinal critter.

When I mentioned this problem to a friend, he asked, "Have you had any cucumbers?" He then told me that the cucumbers from the area cause horrendous gas and that I should pick up some dill seed and have myself a chew. I did what he suggested, and the burping stopped.

Enter the dill pickle. Dill seed was added to pickled cucumbers in an effort to reduce the gas they cause. Recently, cucumbers have been bred to be less gassy. Hence the burpless varieties offered for sale in seed catalogues. Throughout the world, dill is used to quiet the stomachs of people inclined to suffer from gas, and I can testify that it works.

Hiccups are another physical problem tied to stress, and chewing dill seeds is said to cure them almost immediately. My favorite early herbalist, an Englishman named Gerard, had a few words to say about the dill weed in 1597:

The decoction of the tops of dried dill and likewise of the seed, ingendreth milke in the brests of nurses, allayeth gripings and windinesse, provoketh urine, increaseth seed, stayeth the yeox, hicket or hicquet, as Discorides teacheth.

To put that in modern English, Gerard is letting us know that dill seed stops cramps, gas, and hiccups, acts as a diuretic, and increases fertility.

Gerard also mentions using dill to treat a stress-induced condition that

The history of vegetables reads like a soap-opera magazine—who would have thought that the mild-mannered cucumber was once the source of unbearable gas?

most of us don't like to talk about in public: "Galen saith, that being burnt and layd upon moist ulcers, cureth them, especially those in the secret parts." What he is recommending is using the burnt seed of dill as a cure for herpes sores, or as he puts it, "moist ulcers" in "the secret parts." Other herbalists advise taking dill seed tea to treat a flare-up of herpes wherever it may occur. Its soothing nature could well relieve the nervousness which is at the core of an outbreak.

The seed has been an active ingredient in health enhancers since Biblical times. Even so, in those days dill was considered garden trash: several citizens of ancient Israel once insulted a king by sending dill seed as a tribute. This was like sending the tax auditor a baggy of dog dung in lieu of a check for taxes due. Paying the king with dill seed was an affront because the plant grew wild and was about as valuable as dirt. You will not have trouble getting this plant to thrive in your garden!

All you have to do is run out to the grocery store and pick up a bottle of dill seed. It doesn't matter what brand; just get the cheapest you can find. Take the seed home and throw it on the ground in early spring, raking it into the soil. This raking business is critical as birds tend to be hungry this time of year and on the lookout for a tasty, easy meal. Raking the seed underground gets it out of sight and ensures a good crop. Within two or three weeks, the dill will germinate and make itself known, shooting feathery green leaves out from the cool soil.

As to using the dill to relax yourself and increase your vitality, you have two options: you can make tea from either the leaves or the seeds. The leaves can be picked right off the plant as soon as it is big enough to have them. The seeds, on the other hand, appear late in the summer and have to be collected as they turn brown. Add a cup of boiling water to either two teaspoons of the leaf or one teaspoon of the crushed seeds, cover it, steep for several minutes, strain it, and drink the resulting tea before meals.

Dill is not perennial in the traditional sense—the plant itself only lives one year—but it is perennial for all practical purposes. As long as a few of the plants are allowed to remain in the garden to form and spread seed, you will have a whole new crop for the next year. Once again, birds do like the seeds, so you are better off grabbing a seed head and raking the seeds attached to it into the ground at some point in the fall than you are just letting nature take its course. Otherwise the birds may think you left them a winter snack.

ROSEMARY

Like the stomach, the brain is a very important organ regardless of how rarely some people seem to use it, and you certainly want to keep yours in shape. Rosemary is thought both to enhance and to soothe the brain. It's what we might call the "mental overload plant." Contrary to popular opinion, mental overload isn't a new affliction; rosemary has been used to treat it for more than 3,000 years!

In Europe, rosemary has been used as a memory strengthener as well. Traditionally, it was carried and eaten at two critical points in life: weddings and funerals. People at funerals carried it to the graveside so that they would never forget the deceased. Brides and grooms were supposed to eat it and wear it on their wedding day so that they would never forget their vows. Wedding guests were subject to the same treatment so that in the future they would recall that the wedded pair were spoken for.

Rosemary was also burned as an incense at funerals and in

Perhaps the reason marriage is now considered risky business is due to the omission of rosemary from the ceremony. Formerly, no self-respecting bride would have marched down the aisle without it.

sick rooms. Though this custom has largely died out, some Roman Catholic and Eastern Orthodox churches still use the plant as incense in their worship services. The plant was likewise burned in jails to combat "gaol fever," an ancient form of what we now call "kennel cough," except in this case, it wasn't dogs that did the coughing.

Funerals, sick rooms, and jail cells had at least one thing in common: these spots were all packed with disease, and the rosemary was burned there to stop the spread of infection. As rosemary contains bacteria-killing elements, the custom of washing your hands with rosemary water after coming in contact with a corpse, a sick person, or an inmate made a lot of sense. Folks may not have known what bacteria was, but they were keen on the fact that disease spread from one person to the next. Now more than ever, a little cup of rosemary tea might be just what you need, especially after spending the day having bacteria spewed in your face from the office air duct.

On a separate and unrelated, but interesting front, medieval lore had it that in a house where rosemary flourished, the woman wore the pants. Apparently that belief was so deeply entrenched in society that husbands would go out and do a little damage to the rosemary bush if it dared get too big.

Now as to the rosemary in your garden, assuming that it won't threaten your sense of authority, the plant is a native of the Mediterranean, and its very name hints of its sturdiness. Loosely translated, its scientific name, *Rosmarinus*, means "the plant that loves sea spray." Left to its own devices, rosemary will pick a growing spot close enough to the ocean to catch the salty spray on its leaves. Plants that grow near the sea have to be tough—flying sand is more than corrosive. If rosemary can live there, it can certainly live in your backyard.

Starter rosemary plants are available at just about any garden center in the country. Be sure to plant it in a relatively sunny location and in soil that drains. If your soil tends to hold water, dig a hole the size of a watermelon and mix the removed soil with equal parts sand. Put the soil-and-sand mixture back in the hole and plant the rosemary in the middle. Depending on where you live, rosemary can range in size from 12 inches to 6 feet. In colder regions, the plant rarely gets large, and in warmer areas, it will turn into an azalea-sized shrub.

A common symptom of a brain under stress is forgetfulness, and if things just seem to skip your mind, rosemary tea is what you need. Add one cup of boiling water to one teaspoon of leaves. Cover and let the leaves steep for ten minutes, and then strain the leaves. Next, take your tea out in the garden and enjoy.

SAGE

In all European traditions from Ukrainian to Iberian, sage is believed to ensure good health and longevity by gently strengthening the mind and body. The ancients found the herb so capable of healing that they named it *salvia*, "the saving plant." In fact, there is an old Latin saying, *Cur moratur homo cui salvia crescit in horto*, which means: "Why should a man die whilst sage grows in his garden?"

In some parts of France, sage is known as *toute bonne*, or "all good," referring to its general use for whatever ails you. The French believe sage is particularly good for the nerves, the brain, and all that they affect, which is, of course, everything.

Its power to soothe ulcerated skin gave rise to its use in treating boils and problems of the scalp, such as dandruff and scabbing. Sage was also traditionally used for treating ailments of the mouth, from throat conditions to bad gums. (It's interesting to note that gum disease and other skin afflictions are now said to be stress-related disorders.) A gargle of sage tea was recommended for sore throats and was believed to restore the tonsils to good health. The herb has been used for ages to treat bleeding gums, a cure I've personally found most effective. Until very recently, tooth powders, which gave rise to toothpaste, were largely made of sage.

Like rosemary, sage was also traditionally thought to be good for the memory, restoring clarity and quickness of mind. As such, it was used by the elderly to fight off senility. Along these lines, Gerard wrote:

Sage is singularly good for the head and braine, it quickeneth the sences and memory, strengtheneth the sinewes, restoreth health to those that have the palsie upon a moist cause, takes away shaking and trembling of the members, and being put up into the nostrils, it draweth thin flegme out of the head.

Gerard was in good company in his belief that sage would strengthen the nerves—herbalists far and wide say the exact same thing.

Today sage is mostly known as a key ingredient of sausage. Big stands of gray sage appear at country markets in the fall just in time for hog butchering. (Hogs must get nervous when they see it being cut.) The tradition comes from England and the Middle Ages, when sage was popular first in fish dishes and then in sausage preparation. An English cookbook dating to 1393 makes a reference to "Pygges ine sawse sawge." The practice of cooking "pygges" in sage has continued, but unfortunately its head-toning uses have fallen by the wayside. I'd say that it's time to revive them.

As to growing sage, the plant is actually a sub-shrub. This is to say that left on its own, it will become a small shrub. With each passing year, the plant will grow increasingly woody and large. Common garden sage has a silvery green leaf that adds a nice color to the garden. It blooms lavishly, sending up purple shocks of flowers in late summer. A bit hardier than some of the other Mediterranean herbs, sage does best in a sunny location with soil that drains well. Be sure to select a permanent site. Sage is a creature of habit, and unlike some herbs, it really resents being moved. Plant it at the same level it occupied in the pot, water it well for the first season, and you will be in sage for the rest of your life.

Sage plants can be obtained from mail-order companies or bought at a garden center. You can also grab a cutting from a friend. I prefer the old-time sage varieties, and a good way to track one of these down is to frequent farmers' markets and see who sells sage in the fall. Ask one of the vendors to sell you a start. These plants will tend to be stronger in flavor and mind-healing powers than the more modern types.

As to making sage tea, add six chopped, fresh leaves to one cup of boiling water. Remove from the heat, let the mixture stand covered ten minutes, strain it, drink it, and refresh your brain!

LEMON BALM

Thy look of love has power to calm
The stormiest passion of my soul;
Thy gentle words are drops of balm
In life's too bitter bowl.
    —Percy Bysshe Shelley

This mint relation is curious in that its leaves contain the same oils which give lemons their distinctive odor. When you stand on a bed of lemon balm or crush a leaf in your hand, the air fills with a strong lemon scent. Dropped into a tea pot, the leaf gives the water a refreshing lemon taste. As its name and Shelley's lovely little ditty imply, lemon balm is a time-honored soother of mind and body.

John Evelyn said of the herb, "Balm is sovereign for the brain, strengthening the memory, and powerfully chasing away melancholy." In days gone by, "melancholy" was what they called depression, and lemon balm was used to treat both this condition and the feeling of being overwhelmed. Indeed, in European herbalism, lemon balm was used to treat all forms of mental illness and was found to be particularly helpful in cases of what we would now term mental breakdown. Though the plant is good for people who have already gone over the edge, it is equally good for those who just feel it coming, in other words, stressed-out people like ourselves!

In Grieve's herbal, the author tells the story of a man who drank lemon balm tea for 50 years and lived to the age of 116. There are numerous other reports of persons living well past their 100th birthday, thanks to regular use of something called "carmelite water." This was a special tonic made of lemon balm, lemon peel, nutmeg, and cloves. Used from the 18th century forward, carmelite water was an important element in early health regimes. The herbs were ground, mixed with white wine, and allowed to stand for a few weeks. After the mixture was strained, a touch of honey was added. Three teaspoons a day were said to work wonders.

Traditionally, lemon balm has been considered such an inducer of longevity that various herbal physicians have even said that it had the power to bring back the dead. I'm not so sure I would buy that idea, but the herb does seem to perpetuate health in people who use it on a regular basis.

Lemon balm was also used in many societies to scent the house. One must remember that the olden days were also the smelly days. Without proper sewage facilities, cities were pretty rank places, and housewives did everything they could to make their homes smell a little nicer. A custom dating to the Roman Empire, rubbing furniture with lemon balm, remains in a slightly varied form to this day—we still spray our furniture with lemon-scented oils.

Experienced gardeners are always griping about the way lemon balm grows: it spreads like wildfire in a dry forest. But I don't complain about its voracious growth habit. I use a lot of it in my mental-health maintenance program, and given what the modern world can do to a mind, no patch of lemon balm is big enough. Besides, I would rather have to control a plant in the garden than have to coddle it. Buy a starter plant or get a cutting from a neighbor, and you'll be in business. The plant is such a weed by nature that growing it really doesn't need any further instruction—just stick a piece in the ground, and by the end of the season, you'll have a patch.

The scientific name for lemon balm, *melissa*, comes from the Latin *mel*, or "honey." Though the flowers are not much to look at, they produce a tremendous amount of nectar, and any bees in the surrounding area will send out the troops to take advantage of it. The honey made from the flowers of lemon balm is one of the best on the planet, which is something to remember if you are a beekeeper and have a hive on hand.

The best way to use lemon balm for the preservation of mental health is to make a tea of the leaves. I use one cup of lemon balm leaves to two cups of boiling water. Drop the leaves into the pot, remove it from the heat, let it stand covered a few minutes, and then strain the tea. Pour yourself a cup, take it out to the garden, and inhale deeply as you enjoy the tea. By the by, lemon balm does not dry well, so if you want to put some away for winter use, freeze it.

PEPPERMINT

A lawyer friend of mine said something once which I always remember when I think of our next stress-relieving plant. When I asked him how he was, he responded, "I feel like I need a mental mint." Imagine something that does for the mind what a mint does for the mouth! As we all now know, gardening can be just that—a mental mint. For the double whammy, we will include the classic source of mouth refreshment in our list of perfect tonic herbs for the overwhelmed.

Many things we do today on a thoughtless, ceremonial basis have more purposeful roots somewhere else in space and time. An example is the bowl of mints most restaurants have sitting right next to the cash register. Did you ever wonder why or where this idea comes from? What about the mint jelly we invariably serve with lamb? Of all the flavors one could put in the

A stomach is a terrible thing to waste. Fortunately, several plants from the garden can be used to preserve this all-too-often abused and under-appreciated organ.

company of lamb, why is mint so popular? "Yes, I'd like a little toothpaste with my meat, thanks." Well, I'm sure that this one has kept you up at night, and at last your question will be answered.

I've always thought that people used peppermint to hide bad breath. This is true, but people also discovered long ago that eating peppermint after a greasy meal relaxed and soothed their stomachs. Fatty foods are hard for our bodies to digest, but something in peppermint helps to break up the fat. That glob of green stuff to the left of the lamb actually aids your digestion. Peppermint tea, called *poleo*, is still an after-dinner favorite in Spain. People whose troubles sit in their stomachs need to follow the Spanish example. Drop that enervating cup of coffee, which, as a stimulant, is something stressed-out people can do without anyway, and replace it with a relaxing cup of peppermint tea.

The minty toothpaste so common in the current marketplace is also a holdover from days gone by. From the 14th century forward, peppermint was recognized as beneficial to the gums and teeth. Earlier in this century, distilled mint oil was used to whiten teeth, and gargles of mint were made to treat sore gums. The herb has held onto its position as friend of the mouth, and we still see it in toothpastes, mouthwashes, and even dental floss and toothpicks. Unfortunately, most toothpastes today are not flavored with real peppermint, so their medicinal value is nonexistent unless you use one of the natural toothpastes that specify genuine peppermint oil among their ingredients.

Mint gets its name from a legendary source. Menthe was a beautiful nymph favored by the god Pluto. Pluto had an admirer of his own, the goddess Proserpina. Proserpina didn't take to competition, and in an act of nastiness she turned Menthe into a common wayside plant, which was considered quite the insult in mythical days.

There can be no denying that peppermint is a common plant. Originally from the Old World, peppermint happily spread around the globe on the heels of the colonials. The operative word here is *spread*. This is what peppermint will do in your garden, spread from one corner to the other. For the modern gardener, nothing could be better; it's a no-care herb, and it will give you all the stomach- and nerve-settling tea you could ever want. Get a sprig from a neighbor or purchase one from the garden center. Some suggest planting peppermint in a pot to keep it under control, but I couldn't be bothered. The more peppermint spreads, the more I have of it.

The old-time use for peppermint is rather simple. If you have been under a lot of stress and your stomach is upset, or if you have been getting headaches, drink peppermint tea with your meals. Take three tablespoons of fresh peppermint leaves and add them to a cup of boiling water. Take the pot off the heat, cover, let it rest ten minutes, strain the tea, and drink away. It takes a few weeks to notice a substantial difference in your overall well-being, but notice it you will.

HOPS

Have you ever read the side of a can of beer and wondered, what's hops? Well, a hop is the flower head of the hops vine. Dried, these flower heads and the dustlike substance they contain are what is referred to as hops and used in beer production.

The hops vine's botanical name is revealing. *Humulus* comes from the Latin word *humus*, or "rich soil," the type in which the vine prefers to grow. The second half of the name, *lupulus*, comes from *lupus*, or "wolf." The hops plant is likened to a wolf because its vines strangle neighboring plants the way a wolf strangles a lamb. This vining nature makes hops a great addition to a privacy fence or screen. Hops vines grow rapidly. In fact, during the growing season, you can track several inches of growth every day.

The hops is a relative of the stinging nettle and, more interestingly, marijuana. The drug contained in hops, lupuline, is quite similar chemically to the drug contained in marijuana, canibine. The two substances also have similar actions on the human mind and body. Hops harvesters experience a health complication: they fall asleep on the job. This wouldn't be so bad if hops weren't picked on ladders!

Hops is a mild sedative, and people overexposed to it (as in harvesters) have been known to experience breathlessness, cardiac irregularities, fever, profuse sweating, and, of course, sleepiness. Hops dulls the human nervous system, and as such, beer is sedating for more reasons than just its alcoholic content.

Hops has long been used to treat people suffering from nervousness, hysteria, and delirium, all of which are related to an overactive and overwrought brain. This is why I think it's an important plant to grow in our Tonic Garden. Nonaddicting and nonnarcotic, it makes a perfect tea to soothe nerves irritated by a harried modern day.

Prior to the age of sleeping pills, hops was the official treatment for insomnia. It slows the brain that just won't stop going when the body wants to call it a day. There's not much worse than needing a good night's sleep and

NOTHING is worse than insomnia. Thanks to several nonaddicting garden plants, you can kiss those sleepless, stress-filled nights good-bye.

not being able to get it. Many stress sufferers get the mental whirling dervishes just when they should be falling asleep. A cup of hops tea will take care of those spinning thoughts right quick.

One of the old uses of this plant was to stuff a pillow with hops blossoms and sleep on it. Abraham Lincoln, between the American Civil War and his mentally ill wife, had a pretty tough life. He was plagued with terrible insomnia, and when stress took its toll on his sleep, he started using a hops pillow. Fortunately, hops tea is just as effective and lots less noisy.

When you purchase a hops plant, what you really get is a piece of root which when planted will spring into a new vine. One plant will provide more than enough hops for the normally stressed-out family. Toward the end of the growing season, the plant will produce flowers loaded with yellow dust. These are the things you collect to make your hops tea. Be sure not to pick your hops until the yellow dust appears in the flower heads, or you will miss out on the active ingredient. The hops don't keep well in the open air, so I pack mine in empty coffee cans and store them in the freezer.

With my frozen hops in the can, I am prepared for the sort of super-stressful day that makes it impossible to fall asleep. One tablespoon of the whole flower heads added to a cup of boiling water and allowed to steep for ten minutes will do the trick. This tea is so relaxing that it is better left to enjoy before bedtime. That is, unless you have a hammock in the garden, and you want a little snooze under the stars.

CHAMOMILE

Once one of the most popular nerve-settlers around, chamomile tea is making a comeback on the modern scene. Like their grandmothers and grandfathers before them, today's parents are realizing that nothing calms the nerves of an overwrought baby (and her mom and dad) like chamomile tea. The modern world can really work a person over, and some days the best way to describe me is "cranky."

If I had to describe chamomile tea with one word, I would use "soothing." Human beings are thinking animals, and thinking animals need to be soothed now and then. The ancient Egyptians, the Greeks, and the Romans all used chamomile tea to treat the overworked mind. A tenth-century herbal says, "Let hym that hath sore eyes take the ooze of chamaimelon and smerethe eyes therwyth." What the herbalist is talking about is a person so fatigued that his eyes appeared weary, a look many of us sport after a long day.

Three of the most common symptoms of stress are headaches, stomachaches, and skin disorders, and in chamomile, we have an all-in-one treatment should you be triply afflicted. The blossoms have factored into remedies for the skin, taken internally and applied externally, since days predating the Bible. The same blooms are used for headaches and stomachaches, relieving the immediate discomfort and

Stress headaches make you feel as if your head is going to explode. Chamomile can take down the swelling.

the tension which is usually at the root of both complaints.

The flower of this plant is the medicinal part, collected in July at full bloom. Chamomile's scientific name, *Anthemis nobilis*, means "noble flower," and in the heyday of European herbalism, the plant was thought to be just that. Chamomile's common name comes from the Greek word *chamaimelon*, or "earth apple." If you have ever had a cup of chamomile tea, you are aware of its applelike flavor. The Spanish call it *manzanilla*, or "little apple," for the same reason.

One of the problems we modern gardeners have is that we tend to fill our space with organisms other than plants, namely children and pets. Chamomile is the only plant I've come across that actually appreciates being trampled. In *Henry IV*, Shakespeare wrote, "I do not only marvel where thou spendeth thy time, but also how thou art accompanied: for though camomille, the more it is trodden on the faster it grows, yet youth, the more it is wasted, the sooner it wears." Well, you have it directly from Will, "camomille" loves to be stepped on. In fact, in European garden history before grass came into vogue, chamomile was used to make lawns.

Not only does chamomile love being stepped on, it puts out a pungent apple scent when you do. Planting fragrant herbs along the path for the express purpose of getting a nose full of scent while walking along is an old garden tradition now fallen by the wayside. Reviving this practice can make your garden a multi-sensorial experience. It's marvelous to stroll on my chamomile path in late summer with the moon hanging low, taking in the smell of crushed chamomile—a sublime pleasure, if you will.

Chamomile is a short little plant which spreads just like crabgrass. Personally, I would adore crabgrass if you could do something with it—I admire its tenacity. Well, chamomile has all the aggressiveness of crabgrass, but none of the uselessness. I use chamomile for ground cover in my herb bed. It keeps weeds to a minimum and provides a lush green backdrop year-round.

You can use either seeds or plants to start your chamomile bed, but as I myself haven't had much success with the seeds, I recommend that you buy a chamomile plant at the garden center or from a mail-order company. Most garden centers carry the plants in the spring, which is the time to plant them. You will get flowers the first year.

Chamomile blooms in late summer, and every two or three days, I head out to the blooming plants, collect all the open flowers, and freeze them in a freezer bag. You can also dry them quite easily, but freezing the fresh flowers better maintains their amazing flavor.

As to using the chamomile, simply make a tea of the blossoms. Though contemporary people don't tend to practice much preventative medicine, you can use chamomile to prevent stomachaches, headaches, and skin problems as well as to treat them once they've occurred. Generally speaking, these conditions follow a bout of stress. Instead of waiting until you experience the pain, start taking your chamomile tea as soon as you feel yourself getting uptight. Better yet, if you know you are heading into an experience that will work your nerves, take some chamomile tea in advance. A cup of boiling water poured onto one tablespoon of blossoms, covered, cooled, strained, and drunk before meals and bedtime will keep you in good stead.

THE "MY NERVES ARE SHOT" TONIC

In the past, people not only used single herbs as tonics or strengtheners for their minds and bodies, they also used them in combination. In fact, many of our modern soft drinks were originally tonic mixtures made by druggists and served in soda water at the pharmacy. Root beer, for example, was concocted from a collection of roots all noted for their ability to boost the overall health: ginger, sarsaparilla, sassafras, and more.

The contents of our Tonic Garden just so happen to be the ingredients for a healthful concoction you can whip up to keep that old thinker in prime shape. Taken on a regular basis, the "My Nerves Are Shot" Tonic will work against the ongoing damage stress does.

One thing you should understand about tonics is that they work slowly and gradually to improve a person's health and energy level. With them, there is no instant fix. I say this because a lot of people take tonics for a few days and conclude that they don't work. Tonics do work, but they don't work in a few days. They work over time. If you give them the time they need to work, you will discover just how wonderful tonics are and how much better they can make you feel.

1 cup crushed dill seed

1 cup sage leaves

1 cup lemon balm leaves

1 cup peppermint leaves

1 cup chamomile flowers

2 cups lemon peel

2 cups lemon juice

6 cups honey

(If using dried herbs instead of fresh, cut the quantities to ½ cup apiece.)

Add all ingredients except the lemon juice and honey to one gallon of boiling water and simmer for ten minutes. Take the pot off the stove. When the herb-water mixture is cool, strain the herbs out and add the honey and lemon juice. Pour into jars and store in the refrigerator. Take two tablespoons of this tonic before every meal, and in a few weeks you will notice an improvement in your mental strength and stamina.

STRESS-ERCISES

・・・・・・・・・・・ **Preliminary Exercise** ・・・・・・・・・・・

On a little piece of paper, write down all the things that are causing you stress, concern, or annoyance. If some person, situation, or thing is robbing you of your serenity, make a note of it. Once you have written your stress list, go out to the compost pile, which I'll tell you all about in Chapter VII, dig a hole in the compost, and bury the little piece of paper. Once you drop your troubles into the hole, try to leave them there as you walk away.

After you have done the preliminary exercise, choose one of the following and do it every day for a week.

・・・・・・・・・・・ ❧ *One* ❧ ・・・・・・・・・・・

Pick a leaf from any one of your herb plants, sit down in your garden chair, and scratch and sniff the leaf. As you do, concentrate on the odor. Think what it reminds you of. Scratch and sniff the leaf 20 times.

・・・・・・・・・・・ ❧ *Two* ❧ ・・・・・・・・・・・

Get a magnifying glass. Pick three different leaves and while sitting in your chair, examine them carefully, noting their differences and similarities. Fragrances produced in glands on a leaf are sometimes delivered through fine hairs covering its surface. See if you can detect them.

・・・・・・・・・・・ ❧ *Three* ❧ ・・・・・・・・・・・

Gather several different leaves and again while sitting in your chair, pop one into your mouth, chew it up, and savor the flavor. Let the crushed leaf roll over your tongue. It's best to do this exercise with your eyes closed. Compare the flavors of the different leaves.

・・・・・・・・・・・ ❧ *Four* ❧ ・・・・・・・・・・・

Go up to each plant and gently touch it. Shut your eyes and concentrate on the texture of its leaves.

Now for the most difficult prescription. Place your chair in front of your herb garden and stare at the plants for ten minutes. Let your eye travel from one to another. Note any differences in the garden since you last stared at it. Look for insects, watch the plants move with the wind, and notice if one plant is growing faster than another. Most of us are not used to sitting still for this long, so it may be hard at first, but persevere! Peace of mind is only ten minutes away.

MAIL-ORDER SUPPLIERS OF LIVE HERBS:

COMPANION PLANTS
7247 N. Coolville Ridge Road
Athens, OH 45701
614-592-4643

HAVASU HILLS HERB FARM
20150 Rough And Ready Trail
Sonora, CA 95370
209-536-1420

SANDY MUSH HERB NURSERY
316 Surrett Cove Road
Leicester, NC 28748-9622
704-683-2014

WRENWOOD OF BERKELEY SPRINGS
Route 4, Box 361
Berkeley Springs, WV 25411
304-258-3071

SOCIETIES:

HERB RESEARCH FOUNDATION
1007 Pearl Street, Suite 200
Boulder, CO 80302
303-449-2265
(Primarily concerned with medicinal herbs, this group has an interesting quarterly newsletter.)

HERB SOCIETY OF AMERICA
300 Massachusetts Avenue
Boston, MA 02115
617-536-7136
(This group is not concerned with the medical applications of herbs.)

BOOKS:

As with all types of gardening, there are too many books out there to mention. Take yourself to the public library, and you will find more than you could ever read in one lifetime. There is one old standard available, though, which gives the reader a wonderful background in herbs, their culture, and use. The book is entitled *A Modern Herbal*. Written by Maude Grieve, it is a must for every herb gardener. It is actually a two-part set, which you can order through a book store or directly from Dover Publications. The book is fairly priced, and you will get back every penny you spend on it in use.

A MODERN HERBAL
Maude Grieve
Dover Publications, Inc.
180 Varick Street
New York, NY 10014

· · · · · · · · · · · · 🌱 · · · · · · · · · · · ·

CHAPTER TWO

The Scent Garden

When you get right down to it, humans by nature are gluttons for pleasure. If it tastes nice, feels nice, or smells nice, we want more of it. Many a great society has gone down the tubes due to the pursuit of pleasure. In a way, the modern era is the most deranged period humanity has ever experienced: rather than killing ourselves with pleasure, we are killing ourselves with a lack of it. In order to truly pleasure yourself, you have to use your senses, and that is what most of us have stopped doing.

It used to be that people loaded their bodies, their homes, and their possessions with as many good scents as they could afford. Furniture was rubbed with fragrant herbs and drawers and closets were filled with them, bath water was infused with flowers and their essential oils, and skin creams were laden with exotic scents. Today the most popular creams are those that have no smell at all. The other day I saw people walking past an enormous lilac in full bloom, and they didn't even stop to treat themselves to a sniff. This is lunacy. Hold on, poor little nose, we are about to do something nice for you.

There may be more to that old adage, take time to smell the roses, than we think. Scientists are finding out that what goes in through the nose does indeed affect how we feel and how we think. In our next garden plan, we are going to explore our noses, and more to the point, how we can use them to relax and lose our stress. We will be creating our own private aromatherapy treatment center.

You may have seen aromatherapy candles, incense, and bath and massage oils for sale at nature food stores around town. In fact, whole companies are springing up to deal with the demand for aromatherapy products. In aromatherapy, maladies, mental and physical, are treated with smells produced by plants. It may strike you as rather a wild idea, but practitioners of aromatherapy are enjoying tremendous success.

Aromatherapy seems like a new concept, but actually it's not new in the least. People have always gravitated toward good smells and away from bad ones. Good smells make us happy. When a gardenia is in bloom, the aroma draws people to the plant; they go out of their way to breathe deeply the wonderful fragrance. The ancient Egyptian tombs, upon desecration, yielded container after container of sweet-smelling essences placed there so that the dead might continue to enjoy some perfume.

The ancients were much more in touch with scent than we are, and a conversation with an average Joe just a few hundred years ago would have revealed lots of fun aromatherapy facts. In days gone by, people said that the scent of daffodils would cause laziness and insanity and the smell of violets good health and a sense of well-being. Smelling salts were scented with lavender oil because people found the scent rousing to those who felt faint, and the practice remains to this day.

Cleopatra, the Grand Diva of Scent, used fragrance to put men under her sexual charm. She burned incense in her chambers to inflame her lovers with passion, and her scent formulas were said to be so powerful that any man would yield to her once he whiffed a whiff.

The Bible is littered with mentions of sweet-smelling plant products—from cinnamon to frankincense and myrrh—all used in worship services. The Indians and Chinese were equally adept at manipulating emotions through such intoxicating odors as jasmine, honeysuckle, and rose. The ancient Greeks and Romans were similarly involved with collecting plants that put off a heady odor and with using these odors to illicit specific responses.

Can scents really change the way you feel? At a recent dinner party, I decided to burn some frankincense and myrrh to see what they would do to our dinner conversation. As the incense billowed its perfume around the room, a deep glow fell upon the faces of my dinner guests, and we all agreed that we felt much more relaxed and peaceful. This is probably the reason why frankincense and myrrh have traditionally been included in temple rites. Frankincense is still the official room freshener of the Roman Catholic Church!

The idea that smell can affect the mind is getting increasing attention these days. Scientists have recently discovered an entirely new organ located inside the nose. This organ is believed to detect sex pheromones—substances emitted by the body that attract sexual attention. Have you ever had someone drive you mad with passion for no good or apparent reason, even when you didn't particularly like the person or want to spend time with him or her? Researchers feel that such a person is probably emitting a sex scent to which your pheromonal sensory organ is reacting. Sexual attraction may actually be governed by smell.

Pheromones aren't just for sexual communication, though. Scientifically speaking, they are any chemicals put out by one animal and received by another of the same species to convey a nonverbal message. The classic example of this is the congregation of male dogs at your gate when your female dog is in heat. Your female dog has emitted a chemical into the air, sending a silent message to all the other dogs that reads something like this: "Come and get it!"

Scientists had long been aware of pheromones and pheromone receptors in animals. Until recently, however, they felt that this receptor, present in most animals, somehow had disappeared in man. They theorized that it was in place in the embryonic phase of human development but just "went away" as the fetus grew. The conclusion was that we adult humans didn't have a pheromone receptor.

All that changed with the discovery of what has been named the vomeronasal organ, in short, the VNO. Located on the inside of each nostril, the organ is microscopic, but highly functional and quite capable of detecting pheromones emitted through the skin of other human beings.

Have you ever smelled trouble? Have you ever walked into a room where conversation was running smoothly and all appeared to be fine, but you just sensed that something was wrong, and later you found out that your intuition was on the mark? Perhaps that "sixth sense" as it is called is actually the VNO in operation, picking up all kinds of nonverbal messages sent through the skin of other members of our species to us.

So it seems that there is more to our noses than we had originally thought. Who is to say that these receptors don't pick up other chemicals and send other messages to the brain? Perhaps lavender oil does contain a chemical that tells us to "wake up."

If you have ever gotten violently ill from eating a certain food or drinking a certain liquor, you know what happens when you next smell that item. I ate some bad cheesecake once and was sick as a dog, and for years after the very smell of cheesecake made me gag. The summer smells of New York City have turned more than one stomach, including mine. If a given smell can lower your spirits, why couldn't a different smell raise them? If a putrid odor can turn the stomach, why couldn't a pleasant one soothe it?

Aromatherapists insist that smelling, bathing in, and being rubbed with oils scented with certain plants will improve many conditions and the symptoms thereof. In our Scent Garden, we are going to grow the plants with which aromatherapists treat stressed-out people and their ailments. Here's a list grouped according to use.

GENERAL NERVOUSNESS:

hyssop	lavender	lemon balm

LACK OF ENERGY:

basil	lavender	rosemary
thyme		

PAIN:

chamomile	coriander	rosemary

HEADACHE:

basil	lavender	marjoram
peppermint		

DIGESTIVE PROBLEMS:

chamomile	coriander	peppermint
tarragon		

MENSTRUAL PROBLEMS:

chamomile	lemon balm	rose

RESPIRATORY PROBLEMS:

bergamot	hyssop	lavender
peppermint	thyme	

BASIL

When most of us hear the word *basil,* we think of the Roman basil associated with Italian cooking, but there are actually many other varieties, each with its own distinctive scent and flavor. The aromatic herb, which can now be found all over the world, is a native of India. Sacred to the Hindus, the variety called holy basil is so fragrant that its scent is carried by the wind rushing through it. With a row of holy basil planted in the garden, all you have to do is stand downwind on a hot night, and you'll have head-to-toe aromatherapy.

The 16th-century herbalist Gerard said this about it:

The later writers, among whom Simeon Zethy is one, doe teach, that the smell of basill is good for the heart and head. That the seede cureth the infirmities of the heart, taketh away sorrowfulness which cometh of melancholy, and maketh a man merry and glad.

When you are in the middle of one of those stress attacks, wouldn't you give your right arm to be "merry and glad"? Well, apparently basil can do the trick.

Aromatherapists recommend it for depression and mental and physical exhaustion. From the ancient Indians forward, basil has been used to rid a house of bad spirits as well as eradicate any demons that may have taken up residence in one's soul. A marvelous massage oil can be made from the fresh or dried leaves: just add a cup of almond oil and two cups of basil leaves to the blender. It's pesto for the mind, and if there's any left over, you can always make a little pasta.

CORIANDER

The name of this herb comes to us from a rather odd association. *Koris* is the Greek word for "bug." Apparently, crushed bed bugs emit the same odor as the scratched leaf of the coriander plant. If you are not accustomed to coriander leaf, you might find the odor repulsive. It is, shall we say, an acquired smell. However, as with olives and goat cheese, once you learn to like it, you will love it.

Aromatherapists use coriander to treat fatigue and nervous exhaustion—in other words, to help people who find themselves in a run-down condition.

The times when you would rather sit in front of the television and pretend that you didn't hear the door bell ring are the times to start smelling coriander!

Aromatherapists also suggest the insect-smelling plant for chronic illness, nervousness, and pain. The treatment includes scratching and sniffing the leaves, drinking a tea made with the fresh herb, and having a massage with a body rub made by grinding the leaf with some vegetable oil.

CHAMOMILE

Chamomile's aromatherapy use is quite old. From the 15th century forward, European herbalists have recommended chamomile baths as a means to strengthen and heal the mind and body. Ancient physicians knew the connection between the mind and body and felt that an upset mind would lead to an upset body. According to them, chamomile took care of both, getting the patient coming and going.

Gerard said this of chamomile: "The oyle compounded of the floures preformeth the same, and is a remedie against all wearisomenesse, and is with good successe mixed with all those things that are applied to mitigate paine." How do you like that word "wearisomenesse"? That's Old English for "mentally beat up and in a bad mood."

In modern aromatherapy, chamomile is ground with olive oil and spread on the body. It is also made into tea and placed in the bath, and both are considered marvelous ways to settle the nerves and thereby avoid such stress-related illnesses as stomach upset, menstrual problems, and allergies.

HYSSOP

The name hyssop comes to us from the Hebrew *ezob*, or "pleasant-smelling herb." This should be a not-so-subtle indication of the way the ancient world perceived this plant. A number of early cultures used hyssop to treat respiratory complaints as they considered it one of the most powerful strengtheners of that system. Modern aromatherapists agree. Not surprisingly, hyssop is used specifically for problematic breathing, be it due to chronic infections or nervousness.

An interesting note is that proper breathing does in fact affect the way we feel. Shallow breathing causes feelings of anxiety, whereas deep breathing can, as we will learn later on in this chapter, promote calm and a sense of well being. Poor breathing is a common phenomenon in modern society, and aromatherapists feel that hyssop can help a person correct this problem. The plant is best used by scratching the fresh leaves, cupping them in the hand, holding it to the nose, and breathing in deeply. Concentrate on the fragrance and take as much as you can into the lungs. Hold the breath, then slowly exhale.

LAVENDER

Though the modern world has largely forsaken natural perfumes for cheaper artificial sprays, the shocking fragrance of lavender has remained in vogue. Lavender sachets in drawers and lavender blossoms in potpourri bowls can still be found in households around the globe. Unlike such forgotten scents as lily of the valley, musk, and freesia, lavender's strong and complex odor continues to excite people as it has for hundreds of years.

Gerard said of the plant:

The distilled water of lavender, smelt unto, or the temples and forehead bathed therewith, is refreshing to them that have the catalepsie, a light megrim, and to them that have the falling sicknesse, and them that use to swayne much. Lavender helpeth them that have passion of the heart, prevaileth against giddinesse, turning or swimming of the brains, and members subject to the palsie.

I think we can safely assume that he was speaking about anxiety when he suggests using lavender to treat the "swimming of the brains."

Modern aromatherapists find lavender handy for everything from head aches to skin disorders, not to mention infections and irritations of both the respiratory and digestive tracts. The blooms of the plant are used in honey-sweetened teas, added to the bath and massage oil, and, of course, simply smelled.

LEMON BALM

If there ever was a weed in the world, lemon balm would be it. The herb is so invasive that it can be found on the back of commercial herbicides as one of the potential victims. Lemon balm is an Old World plant, highly recognized by ancient Greek, Roman, and Arabian physicians and still prized by modern European ones for its ability to settle the mind and strengthen the nervous constitution.

Gerard quoted another herbalist on using lemon balm as an aromatic:

For Avicen in his book written of the infirmities of the heart, teacheth that Baume makes the heart merry and joyful, and strengthens the vital spirits ... comforts the heart, and driveth away all melancholy and sadnesse.

For people who internalize their stress and wind up feeling depressed, lemon balm may be the smell of choice.

Like the physicians of earlier times, today's aromatherapists use lemon balm as a building agent for the mind and the nerves. They feel that any condition resulting from nervousness, from headache and insomnia to ulcers and depression, is helped with lemon balm aromatherapy.

As we learned earlier in the book, fried nerves are at the root of many of our illnesses, and taking some time to soothe them will pay dividends of good health. The aromatherapists suggest mashing lemon balm with the fingers and smelling it, drinking tea brewed with the fresh herb, grinding the plant with some oil for a scented massage, and, last but not least, boiling a handful or two of the fresh leaves and adding the pot to your bath water.

MARJORAM

A native of Asia and a relative of the even more strongly scented oregano, marjoram has made its way around the globe. Legend has it that the herb was originally scentless until Aphrodite's son was injured doing whatever it was that gods did to get hurt, and Aphrodite used the plant to heal him. Who's to say, but the herb is certainly pungent today. Marjoram is sacred to the Hindu gods Shiva and Vishnu and to the ancient Egyptian god Osiris, and its healing capacities are more than renown.

Gerard was all in favor of marjoram. He notes that:

Sweete marjoram is a remedy against cold disease of the braine and head.
There is an excellante oil to be drawne forth of these herbes, good against
the shrinking of the sinewes, crampes, convulsions, and all aches proceed-
ing of a cold cause.

Stress is certainly what I would call a "disease of the braine," and marjoram's
power in this regard has not gone unnoticed by modern aromatherapists.

They strongly recommend it for fatigue, high-strung nerves, and insomnia. Grind the plant with some almond oil and use it in your bath, or rub yourself with a bit of the same before bed. Some aromatherapists suggest lying in
bed with some marjoram and doing the scratch-and-sniff routine to induce a
deep and peaceful sleep.

PEPPERMINT

Peppermint is a common plant. It's also one of the oldest aromatics around.
It was used by the ancient Israelites and many other early societies to improve
digestion, relieve colds and headaches, and generally stimulate the body's well
being. Our good friend Gerard had this helpful tidbit to say about it:

Peppermint being applied to the forehead or to the temples, as Pliny teacheth,
doth take away the headache. The water of peppermints is of like operation
in divers medecines, it cureth the trenching and griping paines of the belly
and the bowels, it appeaseth headache, stieth yexing and vomiting.

In case you have a bad case of trenching, you will be happy to know that peppermint will take care of it, as well as a nasty bout of yexing, whatever these
two things might be. More common conditions of the modern era, headache
and stomachache, are also eased with the use of peppermint.

In aromatherapy, much as in traditional medicine, peppermint is held in
high esteem for nerves and digestive problems. It is also considered a general
strengthener. Dried or fresh, peppermint makes a great tea and a wonderful
addition to massage oils and bath water. But I think peppermint can be best
used right in the garden by simply sitting in your chair and scratching and
sniffing.

ROSE

No one needs to be told of the intoxicating odor of a rose. Originally from Asia, the rose has spread across the entire globe for no other reason than its beautiful scent. When you go to the garden center to purchase your bush, by all means ask the personnel there which is the most fragrant rose they carry and buy that one. I mention this because many of the new rose varieties have been bred not for scent but rather for shape, and you don't want one of those nonstinkers. Growing roses that don't produce scent is beyond stupid in my estimation.

The ancient writings are a treasure trove for rose facts and uses, and a light perusing will turn up countless references. Since we started with Gerard and his 16th-century aromatherapy suggestions, we will stick with his word on the matter: "The distilled water of rose is good for the strengthening of the heart and refreshing of the spirits, likewise for all things that require a gentle cooling." Rose water may be the perfect item for a person stuck in some dreadful traffic jam. In fact, it may pay to keep a rose in the car precisely for those times when your mind is about to overheat.

In aromatherapy, the rose is considered an all-purpose plant, good for just about whatever ails you. From nervousness to stomachaches, from poor immunity to migraine headaches, aromatherapists see the rose as being something we all need to take the time to smell.

If you have a particularly dismal commute, it might pay to spend a little time in your garden, fueling up on inner peace before you hit the road.

ROSEMARY

Rosemary is one strongly scented herb. Merely scratching a single leaf will make your hand smell like rosemary for an hour or more. This probably explains how ancient man first noticed the plant—all you have to do is brush against a bush, and you walk away wearing its fragrance.

One of the most famous brain-tonic herbs around, rosemary is a great gift to the mentally overwrought (that's people on the edge, if you will). The plant is so powerfully rejuvenating that many old-time herbalists believed adding rosemary to one's health regime could actually preserve youth. According to men and women who knew their plants, a dip in rosemary water would bring someone back from the brink. In aromatherapy, rosemary is also drunk in teas and simply smelled to impart its benefits.

TARRAGON

The French have been tarragon's biggest fans for some time now, and many ancient French herbals sing the virtues of the plant they called *targon* or *herbe du dragon*. Long associated with dragons and other supernatural creatures, tarragon has a reputation in the healing arts suggestive of near-magical power. It certainly is flavorful. However, the frequent use of the herb in French cooking may be due not so much to its taste as it is to the Gallic belief that tarragon is superlative at toning the stomach and improving digestion.

Tarragon is used by aromatherapists for all digestive complaints, problems with which more than one stressed-out person has had to deal. Tarragon tea followed by a rubdown with tarragon body oil is said to put the stomach in a happily restive position, eradicating pain and discomfort. Menstrual irregularities are also believed to give way under the smell of tarragon, particularly when the herb is massaged on the body.

THYME

The name thyme comes from the Greek word *thumos*, or "smell," and if you have ever stood on a live thyme plant, you know why. When the plant is crushed, its odor can float all the way up to the nose. The Sumerians used the tiny herb some 3,500 years ago, and the ancient Greeks and Romans were likewise fond of it and its strong scent. In the 1700s, thyme was used to produce a substance called *baume tranquile*, or the "tranquilizing balm." Thyme applied to the body was said to relax a person and take the brain-ache away.

Back to that old-time aromatherapist, here's what Gerard had to say about thyme and the nose:

Time taken in like sort is good against the sciatica, the paine in the side and brest, against the wind in the side and belly, and is profitable also for such as are feareful, melancholicke, and troubled in mind. It is good to be given unto thost that have the falling sicknesse to smell unto.

Gerard was so convinced of thyme's power to invigorate that he recommended its use to rouse people who had blacked out or fallen into convulsions. I hope your stress problem isn't that out of hand, but should it become so, do try to pass out in the midst of your thyme bed.

Thyme may be just the ticket for the stress gardener who needs a little *baume tranquile* in his life. Aromatherapists suggest using the herb for fatigue and depression, either taken in massage oils or tea or sniffed in the hand.

• • •

All the plants in the Scent Garden are common ones, easily obtained from the garden center. Buy them there, follow the planting instructions, and tend them with care. Rather than give you details on how to grow them, which you can get at the point of sale, I thought we would dive into how to use the plants to relieve your stress load, which is, after all, our most important mission.

In classic aromatherapy, the therapists work with distilled essential oils. The plants are collected in large quantities and steamed to separate the vegetable matter from its fragrant oils. Bearing in mind that it takes several hundred pounds of raw thyme to produce one pound of thyme oil, and several thousand pounds of roses to produce one pound of attar of rose, we will not be producing these essential oils.

We will instead be using the fresh herbs in their raw state, and unless you live in a tropical region, this means that your aromatherapy will have to be confined to months when the herbs are up and standing in the garden. For most of us, this is at least half of the year, so it won't represent any great hardship. If you grow so accustomed to losing your stress through aromatherapy that you can't do without, you can always shift to the commercially produced essential oils when your fresh supply is out of season.

STRESS-ERCISES

Before we get to the exercises and options of working with your aromatherapy garden, we need to cover one basic element in the process of aromatherapy: breathing. Most of us do enough breathing to stay alive, but many do not take full advantage of what controlling our breathing can do for our stress problems.

You may have noticed that when you get uptight, your chest constricts, and your breathing becomes shallow. Some people even experience a feeling of lightheadedness. The mind gets upset and sends a message to the lungs to breath in a way that makes you feel bad.

Breathing is a controllable body function; you can learn to control your breathing and thus control the way you feel. In the aromatherapy garden, you have the opportunity to do precisely that. The best way to breathe for a feeling of relaxation is to take deep breaths, hold them deep in the lungs, and exhale slowly. As you use the aromatherapeutics, bear in mind this preferred manner of breathing. Breathing deeply and slowly will intensify the experience exponentially.

· · · · · · · · · · · **Preliminary Exercise** · · · · · · · · · · ·

While sitting in your chair in the middle of your garden, put your hands on your chest. Inhale to the count of 20, slowly filling your lungs with air. When you have reached the 20 mark and your lungs are full, exhale to the same count. Repeat this exercise ten times before starting any of the aromatherapy options.

· · · · · · · · · · · ❧ *One* ❧ · · · · · · · · · · ·

BASIC AROMATHERAPY

Collect a few leaves from one of your aromatherapeutics. Take them to that same chair, sit down, and scratch and sniff the leaves. Really focus on experiencing the smells and repeat the procedure several times. Concentrate on slowing your breathing down as you sniff. As most of us are out of shape when it comes to using our noses, it may take some practice before you begin to feel the benefits of this exercise.

············ ❧ *Two* ❧ ············

BODY-RUB AROMATHERAPY

As never before, people are becoming aware of the extent to which the body absorbs substances through the skin. If certain heart medications and preparations to help people stop smoking can be administered through the skin, it seems probable that the chemicals contained in massage oils likewise make their way into the body.

In one form of aromatherapy, oils scented with plants like the ones in our Scent Garden are massaged into the body to produce different effects. All of the herbs we will be working with just so happen to be ones which are said to induce relaxation.

In this exercise, you will need to take half an hour for yourself and be prepared to make a mess. You will have to rub scented oil all over your body and allow it to stay there for 20 minutes or so, because the active ingredients need time to soak into your system. You might want to put a sheet on your bed, or get your bathing suit on and your lawn chair out in the ready position.

The way to make body-rub oil is to blend the herb you want to use with vegetable oil (my personal favorite is olive) and a touch of vodka. Take two cups of oil, ½ cup of vodka, and one cup of fresh herb from your garden, toss the three into a blender, and hit "grind." Next, put the mixture into a covered glass container and allow it to sit in the dark for one day so that the oil can absorb the aromatic essence of the plant. Pour it into a sieve to filter the herbal material away from the oil. Store the scented oil in a glass jar in a dark place. This is important as the essential oils are subject to deterioration when left in the light.

As to using the oil, get yourself in a relaxed situation, be it in the garden, resting on your chair, or in a darkened bedroom, lying on your old sheet. Of course, first you need to do your breathing exercises. With that out of the way, it's time to apply the sweet-smelling oil. As you do, massage it in gently,

70

and concentrate on breathing deeply and smelling the aroma. Massage your entire body. Leave the oil on for at least 20 minutes, and then take a nice hot bath. You can play doubles with this game if you like.

············ ❧ *Three* ❧ ············

BATH TONICS

Cleopatra is said to have maintained her incredible beauty by bathing in a combination of goat's milk and scented herbs. The goat's milk is rather hard to come by these days, but the herbs you can get in your own backyard. The Romans, masters of the bath, had more than one recipe for a stress-relieving, aromatic bath. Here's mine.

Take one gallon of water, ¼ cup of olive oil, and three cups of your selected herbs. Put the water and oil in a large pot and bring them to a boil. Remove the pot from the heat, add the herbs, and cover the pot. Let the herbs sit for ten minutes, then add the mixture—herbs, oil, and all—to a hot tub of water. Jump in, relax, and remember to breathe deeply while you soak.

············ ❧ *Four* ❧ ············

AROMATIC HERB TEAS

One of the simplest ways to take in the aromas of these mind-mending herbs is to make them into a tea and enjoy it either out in the garden, in the tub, or while you are getting your herbal rubdown. Bring two cups of water to a rolling boil and take the pot off the heat. Add two tablespoons of the herb in question and allow the herbs ten minutes to settle. Then strain them and drink, taking time to smell the fragrance as you do.

MAIL-ORDER SUPPLIERS OF SCENTED OILS:

AROMA VERA COMPANY
5901 Rodeo Road
Los Angeles, CA 90016
310-280-0407

ORIGINAL SWISS AROMATICS
P.O. Box 6842
San Rafael, CA 94903
415-459-3998

THE ESSENTIAL OIL COMPANY
P.O. Box 206
Lake Oswego, OR 97034
503-697-5992

EDUCATIONAL RESOURCE:

PACIFIC INSTITUTE OF AROMATHERAPY
P.O. Box 6723
San Rafael, CA 94903
415-479-9121

ADDITIONAL INFORMATION ON AROMATHERAPY:

THE COMPLETE GUIDE TO PLANT AND
FLOWER ESSENCES FOR HEALTH AND BEAUTY
Daniele Ryman
Bantam Books
666 Fifth Avenue
New York, NY 10103

CHAPTER THREE

The Flower Garden

There is nothing more fabulous than flowers. Every culture worldwide reveres them and for good reason—they are inspiration and food for the soul. Who knows why, but flowers have the power to change a bad mood to a good one. If you have doubts about this, go buy a couple of roses and present them to the biggest grouch in your neighborhood. I'll bet you anything that he will crack a smile. If stress has turned you into the local Mrs. Crabtree, do the same experiment with yourself.

By the end of the day, most of us have just about had it, and our attitude is, let's say, less than patient, kind, and loving. What we really need at these times is a little floral attitude adjustment. If a bouquet of flowers can cheer you up, just imagine what a whole garden could do. Planting one is the cheapest way to ensure a steady supply of these marvelous mood-altering plant products.

Contrary to popular belief, flower gardening need not be time consuming or difficult.

A bunch of flowers can make the crabbiest person crack a smile—even if the crab happens to be you!

Although I like to garden, I also like to keep the work to the bare minimum. It could be said that I am a lazy gardener. I have been in pursuit of the care-free garden my entire life. The garden plan I am suggesting here is one that I have been working on for 25 years. I believe that I have gotten all the kinks out, and that it is near perfection—a flower garden that needs little or no attention beyond admiring the blooms.

This is the plan I have installed at my house, and let me tell you, my flower garden is the hit of the neighborhood. Each spring people walk by just to stare at all the flowers in bloom and to smell the amazing fragrance that floats off my garden on the breeze. (If you plant enough scented flowers, you can quite literally smell your house before you see it!) People are always commending me for it, and they always say the same thing: "How do you have the time to keep this garden up?" I prefer them to think I am a slave to my garden, but in truth, apart from planting my garden, I don't do much besides the occasional weeding and, of course, flower cutting. The upkeep on this garden plan takes less time than a weekly trip to the florist.

The key lies in the plants that make up the garden. Let me explain how this garden, which is really a collection of plants, came to be. As a child, I was quite the adventurer, always wandering around the woods, hunting box turtles and collecting this plant and that root. One day I made a startling discovery while walking through the woods near my home. It was an old cemetery. Of course, the world is filled with final resting spots, "marble orchards" as my father calls them. What made this one so startling was that it was covered by a sea of yellow daffodils, waving in the cool spring wind.

It was quite a sight. Below the daffodils were peony and iris plants just waiting to push up, garnishing even more radiant blooms. As a young gardener on a budget, I found this unattended plant source much more than exciting. Not only was I an adventurer, I was an adventurer toting pruning shears and a trowel. Getting right down to business, I pulled my tools out of the old satchel and helped myself to a few "starts," or cuttings, of the plants that were blooming so profusely. I carried these cuttings home and put them into my garden. Once in place, they performed as they had done in that long-abandoned cemetery, wildly spreading, providing a marvelous bloom year after year.

Over the course of my lifetime, I have continued collecting flowering plants from abandoned cemeteries and forsaken farmyards. Taking a little start from each site and transplanting it into my garden has resulted in what I call the "no-care flower garden."

In days gone by, people planted graves with real flowering plants, not plastic. Usually this meant a cutting of the deceased person's favorite flower from his or her garden. As such, old cemeteries are repositories for old-time flowers. Once tenderly planted on the final resting place of a loved one, these flowers have continued blooming for decades.

You may have picked up on the significance of this for the modern gardener. Flowering plants planted on graves more than 100 years ago that still bloom each spring with no attention from a groundsperson or landscape crew are plants that essentially take care of themselves.

This is the key to this Flower Garden. The plan I am suggesting to you is made up of these cemetery flowers. Think about it: if these plants continue to grow, flower, and reproduce with no weeding, no fertilizing, quite literally no care at all, just imagine what they can do in your garden. At a bare minimum, they will do as they did in the marble orchard, which is quite a lot. You can throw the "I don't have time to flower garden" argument out the window right now.

The flowering plants found in old graveyards are perennials. As I mentioned in the chapter on the Tonic Garden, a perennial plant is one that comes back each year from the same roots. An oak tree is a perennial. Daffodils are perennial as well; each spring the flowers shoot from the same bulb as they did the spring before.

Annuals are plants that live for one year and then die. As an example, marigolds sprout, grow, flower, produce seeds, and die all in one growing season. Actually, the word annual comes from the Latin *annus*, or "year." The word perennial also comes from the Latin: *per* (throughout) and *annus* (year). Perennials return to life throughout the years.

Annuals are nice, but they come packing a problem: here today and gone tomorrow. If you plant a flower garden with annuals this year, you will have to replant it again next year. When you plant a perennial garden, you plant it once and have flowers for the rest of your life and then some. In terms of both time and money management, it just doesn't make sense to plant annuals. Perennials, the superstars of the graveyard scene, are the ideal plants for the modern gardener.

Now I'm certain that you understand the concept of appreciation and depreciation: cars as they age depreciate, or lose value, and money in a savings account appreciates, or gains value. Well, perennials are plants that appreciate. Once you make the initial investment of purchasing and planting perennials, the plants make returns for the length of time you allow them to remain in your garden. A single tuber of iris becomes two tubers of iris, then four, then six. That field of daffodils in the cemetery that started this garden plan happened because someone planted one or two daffodils bulbs on his mother's grave. Over the decades, the daffodils continued growing and multiplying, creeping from one grave to the next. When you plant a perennial, not only do you never have to plant it again, your plants double and triple in number with each passing year.

The idea of planting a garden is to reduce your stress level, not increase it. With this all-perennial garden plan, the only thing you need to do is weed a little here and there, and your flowers will come back each spring in even greater numbers, providing you with even more awe-inspiring blooms. The concept can be summed up as follows: you sit on your butt while the neighbors ooh and aah.

Back to our not-so-insubstantial stress problem. Many would tell you that the exhaustion you feel is in part a spiritual problem—our modern world exhausts our spirits as well as our minds and bodies. When the spirit grows weary, it's hard to find the energy to get off the couch. Planting this flower garden will do more than reduce your florist's bill, it will give you a sanctuary in which you can rejuvenate your soul. Sitting in the midst of flowers is powerfully healing, and putting this flower garden in place will provide your spirit with the refueling station it desperately needs.

DAISY

Most of the myths about the origins of flowers have a Romeo-and-Juliet touch: someone falls in love with the wrong person, someone dies tragically—you get the picture. Generally someone gets killed in a messy fashion, and the flower springs up from spilt blood.

The myth surrounding the daisy's creation has a clever twist on the usual theme. It goes like this: Bellides, the nymph in charge of meadows, was having herself a solo dance party in the middle of one of the meadows she was supposed to be watching. Vertumnes, god of the orchard, saw her dancing her day away, and decided that Bellides should dance alone no more.

Bellides got wind of his plans through the god-and-goddess grapevine and made other arrangements. As Vertumnes was on his way to collect his bride, Bellides turned herself into a flower. To this day, daisies, or bellides as they are known in some places, can be seen dancing away in unplowed fields.

Daisies have always been associated with love and love magic, used to attract love, repel it, and even foretell it. Remember the "he loves me, he loves me not" routine? This dates back to the days when magic was still widely practiced in Europe, before Roman Christianity ruthlessly eradicated European paganism in the 15th century.

The English word *daisy* comes from the Anglo-Saxon word *daeges-eage* or "day's eye," in what is commonly held to be a reference to the flower's tendency to close its petals at the end of the day like little eyelids and then open them again in the morning. In Welsh, the daisy is known as *llygag y dydd*, which translates as "day's eye" as well.

In the language of flowers, the daisy means innocence. In former times, each flower had a meaning, and sending a bouquet of flowers was like sending someone a coded message. A bouquet of daisies meant "I share your sentiments." If you knew someone had the hots for you, and you wanted that person to know you felt the same way, you'd send a bouquet of daisies with your calling card in it. Faint traces of this old-time language are still kicking around; a bouquet of red roses still means "I want your body," which is what it meant in the old days.

The daisy used to live solely on the European continent and in parts of Northern Africa. Today, its range extends to every continent. From sea to sea, unplowed fields are filled with the nauseatingly cheery bloom.

In Europe, the daisy was a field flower, not a garden flower, meaning that it grew wild without any cultivation. When the English, Scottish, and Irish moved around the globe, they brought the daisy with them. They planted the seeds in their flower gardens, but the daisy quickly returned to the field and has stayed there ever since.

The daisy is a creeping, moundlike plant, with growth habits quite similar to that of its relation, the garden mum. From a central point in the plant's crown spring dozens of shoots that will ultimately hold the blooms. This central mound sends out underground shoots that will resurface in the next growing season to become new colonies. It's in this manner that the daisy has spread from coast to coast, and it will do exactly the same thing in your garden.

DAFFODIL

The daffodil is the quintessential flower of the forgotten cemetery. Like the rest of our graveyard flowers, the daffodil was brought to the New World by European colonists for their gardens, but due to its amazingly vigorous habits, it can still be seen growing in all kinds of wild and unattended places throughout the country. All it takes is one bulb to create a sea of white or yellow daffodils, and there's no nicer way to herald in the spring. No two ways about it, you need to have daffodils in your garden.

The Greek myth about the daffodil's origins is especially interesting. It seems that there was once a most beautiful young man named Narcissus. He was the rage of ancient Greece where everyone admitted to his unnatural physical perfection. Needless to say, this didn't make him terribly popular. The saving part of the tale is that he wasn't pleasant in the least.

Narcissus was quite aware of how good looking he was, and he used it to his advantage whenever possible. In fact, he was so involved with his own beauty that he spent his days sitting beside the water, looking at his own reflection. A maiden from a family with clout fell in love with Narcissus, but because he spent all his time admiring himself in the lake, he never even noticed her. Zeus got tired of Narcissus's self-absorption and turned him into a flower forever nodding at the water's edge, the plant we now call the narcissus, or daffodil.

The plant may have sprung up from a stuck-up little snot, but it serves the modern gardener quite well. The bulb of the daffodil looks like an onion with several smaller onions at its base. These smaller bulbs quickly turn into big bulbs, which in turn produce more smaller bulbs. The cycle repeats itself, and in time the daffodil patch goes from one bulb to thousands. Each bulb produces a bloom, so that the more bulbs there are, the more flowers you will have.

Most garden plants wait around in the cool soil for the warmth of spring to wake them up. Not so daffodils. Rain or shine, cold or warm, they bloom in early April. It's nice to have flowers to cut year-round, and the daffodil helps to extend the season. The plants spring up around the first of March and disappear back into the soil just as the other perennials start their show. In fact, they disappear to such an extent that they can be planted *under* your other perennials without interrupting their growth.

Daffodils aren't just yellow anymore; they come in almost every color under the rainbow. In the breeding process that has produced this variety, some daffodils have lost their scent. As you shop the racks at the garden center, make certain you buy the varieties that are clearly marked "fragrant." You haven't lived until you've smelled a daffodil in bloom.

Many novice gardeners head to the garden center to buy daffodils in the spring. Wrong! They are called fall bulbs because that's when you plant them, not because that's when they bloom. Daffodils are the flower with the biggest bang for your buck. They are cheap, and they guarantee a high return. Remember, every one planted this year will mean four next year!

Planting daffodils couldn't be easier, and there isn't really much to say about it except that the bulbs like to be planted deep, at least six inches under the surface. Stick the bulb in with the pointy part toward the sun. Plant it upside down, and you won't have a daffodil in the spring.

DAYLILY

The daylily is a must for every flower garden, and that's just about all there is to it. No other perennial is as dependable and as hardy. Daylilies grow, bloom, and spread no matter what you do or don't do to them. This is the plant we modern gardeners have been dreaming of—no care and lots of flowers in return. I have a motto when it comes to flower gardening: "If it grows on the highway, I want some." The daylily both is planted and volunteers on highways all over the country. This shows just how perfect it is for the "I'm too busy to garden" set.

Unlike most flowers, the daylily's name is not traced from some great

Greek or Roman myth. Rather, it comes directly from its blooming habit. The individual daylily blossom opens in the morning and closes forever in the evening of that same day.

The daylily we see sprawling from coast to coast is not native to North America. It is an imported plant that merely took the continent by storm. The daylily arrived in the United States with the Chinese laborers brought in to build the transcontinental railroad. They planted it as they moved from one region to the next, and by the time the railroad was finished, the daylily was well established in much of the country.

Though it would be nice to say that the Chinese carried the daylily with them purely for the spiritual inspiration flowers can bring, this is only partly true. To the Chinese, the daylily is both a flower and a source of food. Parts of the plant are edible, and in Asia it is common to take advantage of this fact. If you have ever ordered hot-and-sour soup in a Chinese restaurant, you have more than likely sampled dried daylily blossoms—they're one of the many mysterious articles floating around in there.

Many gardeners object to the idea of using daylilies in the garden because of their roadside history. I think this is just plain silly, but I can go along with people who find the common daylily's color a bit less than pleasing. Personally, I hate orange in the flower garden, and I can assure you that I don't have a single stem of orange daylily in my flower bed.

The daylily is so easily bred that plants are now available in colors essentially ranging from black to white and every shade in between. The colors may vary, but the plant's tenacity in growth and staying power remain unaltered.

The daylily is a grasslike plant that shoots up from a series of stubby, swollen roots which look like long worms with little potatoes hanging off the ends. These roots inch through the garden soil like worms, and every six inches or so, a new plant springs up so that one plant will quickly turn into ten, and so on. As the daylily spreads, the gardener receives increasing numbers of blooms. It's that appreciation thing: plant one plant and in time have thousands. Just remember how the daylily has so happily helped itself to our continent, and picture it doing the same in your garden. There's no such thing as too many flowers as far as I'm concerned.

GARDEN CHRYSANTHEMUM

The advent of the pom-pom mum and its overuse at homecoming games and in inexpensive floral arrangements marked the end of an otherwise very noble plant history. Once one of the most sought- after and dignified of flowers, the chrysanthemum has taken some pretty stiff hits in reputation in the past century. Today, the mum, chiefly known for its appearance in cheap corsages, is definitely a fallen flower. The most regrettable result of this downward descent in popularity is that many a gardener overlooks the chrysanthemum, a plant that performs no matter what and provides the garden with blooms when all else is dead.

Originally from Asia, the mum is thought to have been carried throughout the Western world by some ridiculously early date. Though relics of the flower have been found in many archeological sites across the globe, the Chinese have worked with it the longest (it's first written record in China dates back some 2,500 years), and it is they who are responsible for the modern chrysanthemum. The wild mum is a daisylike plant, hardly notable in any way, shape, or form. When the Europeans were still lumbering about in bear skins, the Chinese were establishing elaborate breeding programs that would stretch and mold the common plant into the thousands of shapes, sizes, and colors that are now available. The first official imperial chrysanthemum competition was held several hundred years before the Roman Empire, and the Chinese remain extremely competitive with their mums to this day.

The flower, with its bright yellow center, looks a bit like a little sun, and in several Asian languages, the chrysanthemum is called "sun flower" or "sun spirit." It is thought to reflect the sun's power and vitality and to convey some of these attributes to whoever grows it. We stressed modern gardeners need all the help we can get, and if the mum only does half of what the Chinese say, it's just the plant for us.

Like the Chinese, the Japanese have had quite a field day with the chrysanthemum, which arrived in their country in 400 A.D. Once there, the already highly cultivated plant was hybridized into even more shapes and sizes. Again it was the favorite plant of the elite, and the common man had little or no contact with it. As in most Asian cultures, the mum symbolizes long life, perseverance, and faith to the Japanese.

The notion is that a person who cultivates chrysanthemums will live a long and healthy life. In the movie *The Last Emperor*, the emperor can be seen tending a patch of mums, a common pastime of the elderly in Asia. As gardening is a proven stress-reducer, there's something to be said for this practice. Some days I already feel as if I am about 85, so I have started tending chrysanthemums now, and I suggest that you do the same.

Mums arrived on European shores in 1689 with trade ships returning from Asia, and they quickly became the craze of the aristocracy. As if the plant hadn't been bred into enough shapes and sizes in Asia, the European royal gardeners took a stab at it and stretched the chrysanthemum even further. Though initially reserved for the nobility, a few mums landed in the hands of commoners, and the easily propagated plant began its descent from royal blossom to prosaic garden flower.

When impoverished Scots sold themselves in exchange for passage to the New World, guess what they brought with them? The chrysanthemum. As these indentured servants planted mums around their new homes, the plant soon became classed as the low-budget posy of domestics. The grand ladies of the colonies turned their noses up at the chrysanthemum and wanted nothing to do with it.

Of course, the last laugh was had by the indentured servants whose mums extended the blooming season of their flower gardens well into the fall. And this remains the flower's chief claim to fame: it blooms when all others have long since retired for the season. In fact, many of the hardier chrysanthemums bloom straight into hard frosts! While the colonial dames were sitting around with nothing but silk bouquets to fill their elegant vases, the indentured servants were still enjoying cut flowers.

There is no more rugged and prolific a garden plant than the mum. It's a spreading perennial which grows in a baseball-diamondlike shape, ever reaching outward. Each year the plant leaps from its fibrous roots and grows into a cascading mound. This mound becomes bigger and bigger until it eventually splits into smaller mounds. These will in time become as large as the original. The chrysanthemum is one of the earliest plants to leaf out in the spring, and as I've said, it's still green and blooming when the killing frosts come.

You can purchase mums at just about any garden center, though the selection might tend to be rather basic. Remember, people have been breeding the chrysanthemum for over 2,500 years, and the list of varieties could occupy an entire library. To get a sense of, let alone obtain, all the kinds available, you will have to contact a specialty chrysanthemum dealer. This is not hard to do. Send for a catalogue—you will be shocked at the number of choices you have.

IRIS

Rainbows are nothing short of breathtaking. I've only seen a half-dozen or so of them in my entire life, and each one has been a wonder, more than enough to stop the busiest businessperson in her tracks. Now, what do rainbows and the common iris plant have in common?

The petals of the wild iris flower, ancestor of our garden plant, contain every color of the rainbow. At first, this might sound a bit tacky, but it works rather well, and the wild iris is as beautiful and dramatic as a rainbow after a summer storm. Noticing this similarity, the ancient Greeks named the plant after Iris, the goddess of the rainbow.

Before perma-glow plastics, people actually planted flowering plants on graves—just a touch nicer than today's practice.

Not only did Iris rule over the rainbow, but she was also thought to carry the souls of departed women to the Elysian Fields, their final resting place. The Greeks believed that planting an iris on the grave of a dead sister or mother or wife summoned the goddess. Though this particular notion had passed long before, the practice of planting iris on the graves of women continued up until the turn of the last century. As a result, iris is one of the plants you will find growing with great abandon in older cemeteries in this country and in many others.

The Greeks were not the only ancient people to notice the iris' shockingly beautiful blooms. To the Egyptians, the iris blossom symbolized power and strength, and they carved it on the tombs of the dead pharaohs to protect them in the afterlife.

It has been the emblem of Gaul since the first century A.D., and the fleur-de-lis, or iris flower, is still the French national symbol. In European flower lore, the three large petals symbolize faith, wisdom, and valor. The great kings of early French history had iris blossoms carved into their scepters and embroidered on their ceremonial clothing.

Wherever the iris grows, people have ascribed magical powers to it, and seeing one covered with morning dew makes it easy to understand why. The iris family is quite large, containing many different varieties. In the modern garden, we have access to Dutch, German, Japanese, Louisiana, and Siberian iris. While all are marvelous specimens and certainly worth a try, the one we will be discussing here is the German iris.

Also known as the common iris, the German iris is so called not because it originated in Germany, but rather because it was first carried to this country by German immigrants. People didn't come to the New World with a lot of luggage, and the fact that they bothered to pack a bit of iris plant is a strong indication of how they must have felt about it. The plants brought from Germany are still flourishing on many an abandoned farmstead and, of course, in the resting places of these early immigrants.

The German iris springs from a bulbous root or tuber. The plant stores energy in this root, and the flowers and leaves shoot from it. The tubers have a creeping nature, and one tuber will quickly become a mass of tangled tubers and green shoots.

To grow iris, your first step is to get your hands on one of these tubers. German iris blooms come in a multitude of colors, shapes, and sizes. Many companies sell nothing but iris, and most of these companies put out beautiful color catalogues picturing the hundreds of varieties now available. The best thing to do is to send for a catalogue and select a few that appeal to you. Do this in the late summer or early fall: you want to order your plants so that your shipment will arrive in early spring. Beyond this, you can either buy a starter plant at the garden center or do a little grave robbing. Ask around the neighborhood—you will probably find someone more than happy to give you a start from his iris clump. Iris do spread, so people are usually more than happy to comply.

LILY

Not many flowers get a Biblical endorsement. In fact, not many flowers even get mentioned in the Bible, with one very obvious exception: the lily. Among the most majestic and awe-inspiring flowers on the planet, the lily more than deserves its place in the Book of Matthew: "Consider the lilies of the field, how they grow, they toil not, neither do they spin, and yet I say unto you, that even Solomon, in all his glory was not arrayed like one of these."

The great news is that to include this hardy plant in your garden you won't have to toil in the least bit. Lilies will effortlessly do all the work that needs to be done. It is one easy plant, but most gardeners forget to include it in their gardens, and that is a royal mistake. Nothing is more glorious than the sight and smell of a lily in bloom—a pleasure we all should experience.

Most of us are only acquainted with the lily as the flower that appears in churches and at grocery stores around Easter time. Its association with the Easter service is actually not due to Christ's obvious familiarity with the magnificent plant. Instead, it dates back to the spring fertility rites of pagan Europe.

The word *Easter* is derived from Eastra, the Teutonic goddess of spring whom pre-Christian Europe honored in a day of celebration. As the fields burst into bloom, people gathered great bouquets of flowers. They brought them to special altars to honor the goddess who had successfully fought the winter off, rolled the cold away, and restored warmth to the earth. Once the honoring was done, the lads and lasses dropped their knickers for what we might call Eastra brunch.

The early Europeans had been practicing certain religious ceremonies for centuries, and they were not about to give them all up when the first missionary banged on their door, offering the infamous option plan: Christianity or death. In many instances, the pagan rituals just got rolled into the Christian holidays, and this is the case with the festival of Eastra. The name got changed to Easter, but flowers are still part of the celebration. Instead of worshipping Eastra, Jesus Christ is so honored. People may have stopped taking their drawers off on Easter Sunday, but they still drag white lilies to the altar.

The lily plant springs up from a bulb closely resembling an artichoke. The stalk appears in the early spring and shoots up to the sun rapidly until it hits its ultimate height in late June. At this time, flowers develop at the top of the shoot. Care must be taken that the shoot is not trampled. Each bulb makes only one annually, and if it is broken off, you lose the bloom for that year. So tread carefully in the lily patch.

When you buy your lily bulb, make certain that you only purchase lilies in boxes marked "fragrant." Several varieties sold, including the white one used for Easter, barely have any smell at all, and the true joy of lilies is their scent.

If the truth be known, unlike our other flowers of the abandoned cemetery, the lily is a little deficient in the foliage department. It's not that the plant is unattractive, it's just that there isn't much to it. Aside from its stately and deliriously fragrant bloom, the lily is only a stalk. The thing to do is to plant it in the middle of your daylilies, which have a much more impressive show of green just about year-round, and enjoy the lily when it's in flower. It's not as voracious a grower as some of our other perennials, but it will maintain itself nicely, multiplying in time.

PEONY

The peony is one of the oldest flowers in both the European and the Asian garden. Its place in the European flower garden predates Christ by several centuries, and on the Asian continent, it was first grown by the Emperor Shin Ming during his rule from 2737 to 2697 B.C. Wild peonies are still found in the forests of the Yunan province in China, and the fact that the plant was hand carried from remote China to the ancient cities of Europe so long ago indicates how beautiful people found its blossom to be.

The peony's name is rooted in Greek legend. Paon was so gifted a healer that he could bring the dead back to life. Needless to say, his services were in demand. His skills made the deceased and their families quite happy, but they angered the god of the dead. He wasn't thrilled to have Paon robbing him of clientele, and to protect his business he plotted the good doctor's murder. From Paon's spilt blood came the peony plant. In Western societies, the peony has been relegated to the garden, but this myth speaks of a time when the peony was equally known and used as a healing plant.

In the days before the extermination of European paganism by Christianity, magic was a big part of the daily course of village life. Putting hexes on people and having them removed was nearly a full-time job, and the peony was used to ward off evil spells, bad luck, and the like. Merely having one planted in your garden was said to offer protection to the entire household. The seeds were collected, strung into necklaces, and placed around the necks of infants to safeguard them from illness and death. Wearing a peony could prevent someone from putting a love spell on you, and stowing a few seeds in the luggage of a traveling spouse was said to ensure his or her fidelity. Beyond this, Europeans used the peony in all sorts of medicine as it was generally considered to offer the body protection against disease.

Although we have stopped using the peony for medicine and magic, the Chinese have not. In China, the peony is a favorite plant used in treating female complaints and rundown conditions. The written record of this dates back 4,000 years, and to this day the Chinese feel that the root of the peony plant powerfully improves the overall health. One belief holds that women who drink peony tea, usually mixed with a bit of licorice, are able to maintain their beauty until the day they die. I'm not sure how thoroughly this particular theory has been tested, but the plant's use as a general strengthener has been born out in scientific studies.

I can't speak of the peony's magical power firsthand, but growing it in the garden I could talk about all day. The peony springs from a series of thickened roots that lie just below the soil's surface. As these thick roots are very brittle and apt to break apart during transplanting, peonies resent being moved. The magnificent peony displays one sees in older gardens result from clumps that have been left in the same spot for at least four years running. Your objective in planting a peony is to pick a spot and leave it there forever.

WOOD HYACINTH

The wood hyacinth is one of my favorite early spring flowers, an old-fashioned classic that has all but been forgotten by the current generation of gardeners. You may not even be familiar with the plant—it's readily available from the Holland bulb growers, but it's one of their best-kept secrets.

Through its name, you may have deduced that it is a hyacinth. Most of us know hyacinths as those lollipops of color that sit in the garden like day-glo plastic Easter eggs. They offer marvelous fragrance, but aesthetically speaking, I think they leave a lot to be desired. This is not the hyacinth to which I am referring.

The wood hyacinth is the wild parent of this overdone child. In its more natural state, the hyacinth is a plant of wondrous beauty, simple yet perfect. Though the plant has a delicate beauty, the myth surrounding its creation certainly doesn't. It would seem that Apollo, god of music and more, had a boyfriend by the name Hyacinthus. And I do mean boyfriend, for the two were lovers. Apollo and Hyacinthus spent all their time playing and hunting in the fields and forests, taking breaks from the summer's heat with occasional nude swims in available rivers and lakes. Apollo's affection for Hyacinthus bordered on the obsessive—he never let the young man out of his sight. One day the two lovers were out tossing the discus around an open field. Apollo made a toss, the wind caught the discus and blew it in the direction of Hyacinthus, and, you guessed it—the discus walloped Hyacinthus in the head, his life and blood were spilled, and from the latter sprang the hyacinth.

The story has a twist. Apparently this death was no accident at all. Zephyr, the god of the winds, had the hots for Hyacinthus and upon realizing that he would never have the object of his desire, Zephyr had the youth knocked off. Love can be so ugly.

The wood hyacinth is a sure winner in the garden, even if it did spring from misfortune. The plant grows from a pearl onion-sized bulb that likes to rest about four inches below the soil's surface. At the base of this "onionette" form smaller bulbs that in time will also bloom, thus forming a blooming carpet. The process continues, and each year that passes will result in an ever-spreading mass of spring blooms.

• • •

Now that you have gotten to know the players in my own little "cemetery plot" Flower Garden, it's time to start talking about weaving them into a floral carpet. The key to a good perennial garden is in the placement of the plants. We are not planning a row of soldiers, but rather a community that works together to create a total impression. If you plant the plants close together, they will form a blooming tapestry, and there won't be any room left over for weeds.

You can purchase the following plants at the garden center all year long: daisy, iris, daylily, peony, and garden mum. Just stop by and get what you need. Of course, the garden centers are best stocked during the spring, so this is probably the best time to do your shopping. It can be pretty slim pickings by August.

These plants must be purchased in the fall as this is when the plants become available for sale: daffodil, lily, and wood hyacinth.

Once your flower garden has been installed and is growing, it is time to include flower power into your stress-reduction regime. As they say, take time to smell the roses, and this is just what you need to do. When the flowers start coming into bloom, go out to the garden, sit down in your garden chair, and watch them for 20 minutes each day.

It has become common knowledge that stressed-out people are really helped by meditation. The only problem is that most of them don't know how to do it. Mention meditation to lots of people, and they immediately envision sitting with their legs strapped over their head. But you don't need a contortionist's body for the kind of meditation I'm talking about. With your flower garden installed, you have everything you need to start. Spend some time in the garden remarking on the beauty of your flowers, and you will be meditating.

STRESS-ERCISES

·········· Preliminary Exercise ··········

Before you dump your stress in your flower garden, you need to do a warm-up routine. In this case, you need to spend ten minutes watering the flower bed. Turn the water on and water each plant individually. Then do some group sprays. Every gardener has his own watering style, but you should get the ground good and drenched. With that accomplished, do one of the following exercises.

Look at your flowers. Don't just glance at them. Really stare at them and learn how they are constructed. Notice what colors the petals are, what the insides of the flowers look like, how one color bleeds into the next. Have your handy magnifying glass out and use it to scrutinize the flowers.

············· ❦ *Two* ❦ ···········

Smell your flowers. Do some deep breathing, slowly inhaling the fragrance and slowly exhaling. It's helpful to close your eyes as you are inhaling so that you focus entirely on taking in the scent.

············· ❦ *Three* ❦ ···········

Take a pair of shears out to the flower garden, create a lovely bouquet, and give the flowers to a friend who is feeling down in the dumps or to one of your neighbors for no reason at all. It will make them feel better no matter what, and it probably will do the same thing for you.

Skip the sci-fi and fantasy novels. Getting up close and personal with a flower proves that truth really is stranger than fiction.

MAIL ORDER-SUPPLIERS OF BULBS:

BAKKER OF HOLLAND
U. S. Reservation Center
Louisiana, MO 63353

PETER DE JAGAR BULB COMPANY
P.O. Box 2010
188 Ashbury Street
South Hamilton, ME 04350
508-468-4707

MAIL-ORDER SUPPLIERS OF PERENNIALS:

BLUESTONE PERENNIALS
7211 Middle Ridge Road
Madison, OH 44057
216-428-7535

BUSSE GARDENS
13579 10th Street NW
Cokato, MN 55321
612-286-2654

ANDRE VIETTE FARM & NURSERY
Route 1, Box 16
Fisherville, VA 22939
703-943-2315

WHITE FLOWER FARM
P.O. Box 50
Litchfield, CT 06759
203-496-1661

MAIL-ORDER SUPPLIERS OF DAYLILIES:

AMERICAN DAYLILY & PERENNIALS
P.O. Box 210
Grain Valley, MO 64029
816-224-2852

B & D LILIES
330 P Street
Port Townsend, WA 98368
206-385-1738

DAYLILY DISCOUNTERS
One Daylily Plaza
Alachua, FL 32615
904-462-1539 or 800-DAY-LILY

MAIL-ORDER SUPPLIERS OF IRIS:

AITKEN'S SALMON CREEK GARDEN
608 NW 119th Street
Vancouver, WA 98685
206-573-4472

ANDERSON IRIS GARDENS
22179 Keather Avenue North
Forest Lake, MN 55025
612-433-5268

MAIL-ORDER SUPPLIERS OF CHRYSANTHEMUMS:

HUFF'S GARDEN MUMS
P.O. Box 187
Burlington, KS 66839-0187
800-279-4675

KINGS MUMS
P.O. Box 368
Clements, CA 95227
209-759-3571

MUMS BY PASCHKE
12286 East Main Road
North East, PA 16428
814-725-9860

CHAPTER FOUR

The Fruit Garden

A walk through literature dating back to the ancient Egyptian, Israelite, Greek, and Roman days will turn up a million references to fruit. Women are likened to peaches, men to figs, and life to an orchard. In the Old Testament, God threatens people by saying, "If you don't act nice, I will make your fruit trees barren." Personally, I would have shaken in my boots at that one! In the Arabian peninsula, the ultimate act of war was to destroy the fruit trees of your enemies. (This was considered worse than raping the women, which they also did.) The Romans and Greeks alike made constant references to fruit: how to eat it, the best time to pick it, and more. People have always adored fruit; some cultures even worshipped the trees that produced it.

After a stroll past the fruit section at a grocery store, contemplating the ancients' love affair with fruit may leave you perplexed. The fruit available to us today is so bad that it's often not even worth eating, let alone worshipping. It's usually flavorless and generally unappealing.

There is an entire generation out there that doesn't like fruit because all they have ever experienced is the less-than-mediocre

Nothing can compare with the taste of ripe fruit, a guaranteed pleasure when you grow it yourself.

stuff available at the grocery. Why would kids like fruit when what they have tasted is so horrendous? Perhaps you yourself don't care for fruit because the store-bought kind is all you have ever known. Well, let me tell you this, these little products of trees, shrubs, and plants can be so delicious that the mere placing of one on the lips can send electric shocks up and down the spine.

You see, a fruit is an evolutionary strategy designed to assist a plant in spreading its seed. An apple is really a seed vessel; the delicious fruit surrounding it acts as an insurance policy for seed dispersal. Animals—that's us—like the fruit around the seed, so we grab it, eat the sweet part, and toss the seed away. In theory, the seed then hits the ground and grows.

As plants fill their fruit with sugars and flavors solely to attract us, they do so when attracting us will do them the most good. That's at the very last moments of the ripening process, when the seeds are mature and ready for planting. Unfortunately, the same sugars that make fruit so appealing make it soft, mushy, and highly perishable. Ripe fruit does not transport well.

The problem comes when the fruit you buy in Philadelphia was grown in Argentina. Obviously, it's impossible to ship a soft, mushy fruit all that way. But if you pick the fruit *before* it gets soft and mushy, when it's still green and hard, you could probably dribble it like a basketball up from South America, and it wouldn't even bruise. So that's what the commercial fruit producers do—they pick before the fruit is ripe.

Of course, green oranges and strawberries don't sell too well at the market, but the same people who pick the fruits before they are ripe have a solution to the green-fruit problem. They pack the immature fruits into a gas chamber and soak them in gases which change their green color to a theoretically better shade (hence those pinkish tomatoes that even the most obtuse consumer recognizes as looking unnatural).

The fruit may look good, but it sure doesn't taste that way. Though it's semi-appropriately colored, it isn't appropriately flavored because Mother Nature wasn't finished with it when it was picked. This is why fruit at the market tastes like nothing—it is nothing. These days the only way to taste a fruit with the marvelous and mysterious essence vine-ripening imparts is to grow it yourself.

Fortunately, this is remarkably easy. Contrary to popular belief, growing fruit is one of the simpler gardening endeavors. Part of the reason it's so easy is that plants are completely geared for procreation: they function with this aim only. An apple tree's entire impetus is to produce apples. You couldn't stop the tree from setting blooms in the spring if you wanted. To create a fruit garden, you need only to plant the plants that want to produce fruit, then sit back and watch them fulfill their biological imperative.

Growing a fruit garden is not difficult. What is true is that some fruit-producing plants require more time to produce fruit than others. Watermelons, honeydews, and raspberries, for example, will produce fruit the first year, while apple trees take five to six years to bear.

Our Fruit Garden is modeled after one of the many small, but highly productive, orchards I have admired in countries around the Mediterranean Sea. It even includes a grape-covered arbor under which you can take your Sunday lunch in the shade. As you may have gathered from the mention of the word *orchard*, this Fruit Garden will be a mix of instant-gratification and longer-term investment plants. I know gardeners suffering from stress like to enjoy their pleasures sooner rather than later, so I will make certain you can pop some really decent fruit in your mouth the first year out. This will tide you over while you're waiting for the other plants to pay off.

APPLES

In the United States, when we want an apple tree for the garden, we either head to the garden center or get out the mail-order catalogue. Believe it or not, though, there is another way to obtain an apple tree. All you need to start your own orchard is probably sitting in your garbage pail right now. Just bury an apple core, and there you'll have it—what I like to call a "crapshoot" apple tree. Read on and you'll see what I mean.

My fascination with gardens started early. I had my first at the age of two. My grandfather helped me plant it, and by the age of five, I could be found curbside dispensing gardening tips to the neighborhood ladies. Somewhere in my first years of public education, my ears pricked as the teacher spoke of Johnny Appleseed planting apple cores from coast to coast, seeding our infant nation with the fruit that would come to epitomize Americana. Most of the students couldn't be bothered, but I listened with fascination. As soon as I

The seeds in every apple can produce apple trees. Johnny Appleseed knew this—what happened to us?

heard that I could start an apple tree with an apple core, I had it in mind to go home and plant one. If Johnny could do it, so could I.

Across from my house lived a retired couple who spent their golden years gardening. When most children were playing cowboys and Indians, I was over at my neighbors', learning more about my favorite occupation. After that fateful day in public school, apple cores in hand, I popped over to my mentors' house for some advice on planting my soon-to-be apple orchard. I was quickly informed that it wouldn't work. Crestfallen, I tossed the apple cores in my friends' compost pile and headed home.

My young mind was perplexed, and it stayed perplexed for some time. When I received my first gardening book for a birthday gift, I was quick to look the topic up. The book, entitled *10,000 Garden Questions Answered by 20 Experts*, had this to say about my query:

Nearly all of our fruits are of complicated parentage, so that when seeds are sown all sorts of variations may be expected to occur. Often the weakest qualities of a genus shows up, or susceptibility to disease.... Very few seedlings are superior to their parents.

My neighbors were backed up by the experts, not just one, but 20! As I grew up, I continued to look into the matter only to read and be told the same thing over and over again: you can't grow apple trees from apple cores. In fact, I have read no fewer than 100 gardening books and found the same notion repeated consistently. Still, as many times as I got the thumbs-down signal, it never made much sense.

What the experts were really saying was that planting apple seeds would lead to a crapshoot—the baby apple tree might produce better apples than its parents, or it might produce worse. Make no mistake, when you plant an apple seed, you will get an apple tree and it will produce apples. It's just that the experts are of the opinion that the crapshoot of planting an apple seed is not in the favor of the gardener.

Some years later, while working on an article on kiwi fruit, I came across a most interesting piece of information. The juicy tidbit surfaced while I was speaking to the director of public relations for the New Zealand Fruit Company. She mentioned that New Zealand produced apples as well as kiwis, and that the Granny Smith, my favorite apple, was a "chance seedling" that had popped up from an Australian compost pile. (By the by, chance seedlings are seedlings that come up by chance, not through a scientific plant-breeding program. They result from planting the contents of an apple core.)

I hung up the phone and knew that Johnny Appleseed was about to be vindicated. I looked into the topic a little further and discovered that, contrary to popular belief, planting apple cores has produced some pretty amazing results. In fact, not only did the Granny Smith originate as a chance seedling, so did the Red Delicious, the Golden Delicious, the Jonathan, the Mackintosh, the Rome Beauty, and the Newton Pippin.

Now you tell me, do you think it pays to plant a few apple cores? Before you answer that question, you should know that Washington State apple growers make $742.5 million a year selling chance seedling apples, and a big chunk of the nearly ten billion pounds of apples produced in the United States grow on chance seedling trees.

So why do the experts suggest we *not* plant apple seeds? As my first gardening book indicated, most of our fruits are of complex heritage. When you plant a seed, you simply don't know what will come up. Just like you and me, the Granny Smith apple has four grandparents. If the Granny Smith flower is pollinated by Mackintosh pollen, the resulting seeds will have eight great-grandparents. When the seeds are planted and grow into trees, the trees could produce fruit that takes after any one of the parents, grandparents, or great-grandparents.

To put this in perspective, let's look at something we are all familiar with. The laws of genetics apply to fruit trees and people alike. Children tend to resemble parents more than they do their grandparents, and my experience has been the same with fruit trees. The truth is that when you plant a seed from a fruit in hand, you don't know exactly what you are going to get, but if you plant a seed contained inside a Granny Smith, it's safe to assume that the seedling will resemble the Granny Smith parent. Even if the seedling is a throwback to a great-grandparent, it's likely to produce a decent apple.

In any event, all eight great-grandparents were orchard apples, so the chance of ending up with a crab apple is pretty slim. I think the chancy nature of planting seeds makes it fun. How exciting—you have no idea what kind of apple will be born from the tree you started from seed.

Bear in mind that the apple falls not far from the tree. You don't want to plant seeds from just any piece of fruit; you want to plant seeds from the best piece of fruit you can find! Don't go on appearances. A big shiny apple may have no taste. The best way to get your seed for planting is to save one from a piece of fruit you thought had exceptionally good flavor. Plant it, and it will produce a tree likely to bear fruit with similar attributes.

Not all the seeds in a fruit contain an embryo—some are duds. Before you start the process of planting seeds, you want to make certain the seeds contain something that can sprout. The rule of thumb is: live seeds sink in a glass of water. Throw away the seeds that float.

After you've selected your parent fruit, carefully take the seed cask apart, remove the shiny blackish-brown seeds, and conduct your embryo test. Then fill a coffee canister with clean sand and bury the seeds in it. Place the coffee can in the refrigerator and leave it there until the next spring. The seeds need to be refrigerated for at least a month, so if you are planting the seed from an apple imported out of season, bear this in mind.

In early spring, fill a pot with peat moss and transfer the seeds from the sand into the pot. Bury them one inch below the soil's surface, moisten the peat moss, cover the pot with plastic wrap, and place it in a partly sunny location in the garden. The seedlings will appear within the month. Keep the seedlings potted until late in the fall, and after the leaves have dropped, plant the seedling trees in their final locations. Very few of these fruit trees are naturally dwarf, so you can expect to have a standard-sized tree.

Now here comes the hard part, that waiting game. It takes apple trees between four and eight years to start producing fruit, so this is not an instant gratification activity. Just remember as you watch your apple tree grow that when it does bear fruit, you could have in your own backyard the next Granny Smith or Red Delicious. The apples of each tree are totally distinct from those of even its sibling trees. At a bare minimum, you will have an apple tree that produces apples, and apples that no one else in the world can grow.

MELONS

Melons are the instant-gratification portion of the show. You plant the seeds, and in two months you have mouth-dripping, sweet, tangy fruit to eat. Two months to bliss—that's pretty good, if you ask me. The best part is that you don't have to go to the garden center or send away to a mail-order company to get these plants started. Just run to the grocery store, buy a piece of melon, scoop the seeds out, and you have everything you need to start your melon garden!

This section of the fruit garden is simple enough for a young child. In fact, if you have any in your household, it may be the perfect garden project for them. Getting them started on *some* garden project, by the by, is a good idea—lots of children today are growing up out of touch with nature and the peace it can bring.

A melon vine is like something from a science fiction movie—plant one and you'll see what I mean.

Though I am not a child anymore, I have the patience of one. That is to say, I have none. Things that take a lot of energy and don't give some sort of satisfaction back immediately bore me. Growing melons is a fast operation and one that is immensely satisfying.

A remarkably large number of people don't like melons, and if I was raised on the pathetic bits of colored styrofoam passed off as melons at the grocery, I wouldn't like them either. I refuse to buy commercially grown melons because the air I breathe has more flavor than these insipid fruits and because I know how wonderful the home-grown variety can be.

The reason melons at the supermarket are so wretched once again ties into the current agricultural process. Melons above all fruits get mushy and perishable when properly ripe, and that's a state that doesn't lend itself to international and bi-coastal shipping. Commercial melons are picked as green as can be, long before the plant infuses them with flavor. If you want to enjoy the electrifying experience of eating a vine-ripened melon, it's time to plant your own.

Along with watermelons, we are going to grow honeydews and cantaloupes in our Mediterranean fruit garden. This is quite appropriate, as they are popular summertime fruits all around that area. In fact, the word *cantaloupe* comes from Cantalupo, a region in Italy noted for its marvelous cantaloupe production.

Both the cantaloupe and the honeydew are said to be native to Persia, now called Iran and a country famous to this day for its marvelous melons. A very ancient fruit, melons have more than one mention in the Bible and other ancient texts. Apparently, during the debauched days of Rome, melons (along with every other sensual experience) found great favor. For whatever reason, however, their popularity in Europe died out with the waning of the Romans and their marvelously wicked ways.

Melons were all but forgotten until the 15th century in France when they became so popular that Louis XIV had them grown under glass at Versailles, enabling the pampered noble to enjoy cantaloupes year-round. The cantaloupe made its way to America with the Dutch and was sighted at farmers' markets in the colonies as early as 1653. No fruit was better suited to a people on the move. The colonials didn't always stay in one place long enough to establish fruit orchards, but they did have enough time to plant melons and reap the rewards.

You may have noticed that some people call cantaloupes muskmelons and vice versa. Actually, there is a difference between the two. Muskmelons have the netted skin and cantaloupes the smooth. Both have bright orange flesh and a green rind. In terms of flavor, I can't tell one from the other and doubt you can either. Along these same lines, though honeydews and cantaloupes appear to be quite different fruits, they are so genetically similar that they interbreed easily. Grow these two melons in close quarters, and you'll end up with seeds that have a cantaloupe as one parent and a honeydew as the other. The net result is a whole new line of melons with a taste and physical characteristics somewhere between the two.

The watermelon is indigenous to Africa and can be seen growing wild in the jungles there. In its native land, the fruit comes in just about every shape and size, as small as a grapefruit and as large as the killers we see in our grocery stores here. As with the melons of the Arab lands, every village has its own favorite variety. The flesh of the watermelon can be red, pink, white, or yellow. The longer human beings cultivate a plant, the more varieties pop up, and the many centuries people have been working with the watermelon have left us with a rainbow of choices.

The watermelon spread from Africa to the far reaches of China long before the time of the Romans. Mentions of the fruit appear in all of the earliest written records, including the Egyptian hieroglyphics and the ancient Chinese medical texts. In fact, many an Egyptian tomb has been opened to reveal big piles of watermelon seed! When roasted and salted, they make a tasty, high-protein, high-vitamin snack which is sold at farmer's markets around the world.

Planting melons couldn't be easier. As I mentioned before, you don't even have to go to the garden center to get your seeds. Just save a few from a melon you buy at the grocery. Plant them just after the last frost is due in your area— they're from tropical regions, after all, and are not inclined to take the cold well. You'll only need about six seeds as each will produce a vine that can yield up to ten melons, and 60 melons is enough for anyone.

As you might imagine, a tiny seed that will go on to produce 30 feet of vine and ten-pound melons requires a lot of food. When planting melons, take care of this up front, by making what we gardeners call "melon hills." Take a 50-pound bag of manure and spill it out into a pile. Then dig under the pile to introduce some garden soil. Chop the garden soil into the manure until you have a ratio of one-part manure to three-parts garden soil. Then smooth the mound into a hill and plant three seeds in it. Water them and wait.

One thing we haven't covered with this melon business is the fact that melons, like cucumbers, are vines, which means they spread out on trailing runners. You have two choices in this regard: you can let them grow on the ground, or you can let them grow over a trellis. Since most of us are gardening in a limited area, trellising offers us a space saver. (Although if you grow watermelons, you might want to keep them on the ground.) Take your pick. The melons don't mind where they vine as long as there is space for them to do it.

RASPBERRIES AND BLACKBERRIES

In recent years, raspberries and blackberries have become a treat enjoyed only by those willing to let go of a big chunk of change for the experience. The little berries are one of the most expensive items per pound at the grocery store. This is in part due to the fact that they are among the only decent fruit there.

As the berries can't be picked green and gassed, they have to be vine ripened, which is why they taste like fruit and why they are so pricey. (It costs more to get ripe fruit to the market than golf balls.) The good news here is that for the price of one pathetic little box of raspberries, you can buy ten raspberry bushes which will produce so many gallons of raspberries that you will have no choice but to make jelly and jam.

Like many of our fruits and vegetables, the raspberry has a rich and interesting history. Did you know that raspberries were used to flavor Dr. Pepper? Have you ever wondered what those purple USDA stamps on meat are made of? Well, it's blackberry juice!

Blackberries and raspberries are closely related plants from a famous family that includes the rose. Scientifically speaking, the difference between a blackberry and a raspberry lies in how the fruit hangs on the bush, or, in this case, doesn't hang. Raspberries pull off the vine, leaving the stem, and blackberries pull off the vine, retaining their stem. Apart from this, they are genetically quite similar, so much so that they can interbreed.

Prior to the age of colonization, Asia, Europe, and the Americas all had their own unique blackberries and raspberries, but with international trade, European and Asian berries ended up in North America. When birds ate the fruit of imported European and Asian plants and voided the seeds, the plants escaped into the wilds and mated with the local berries to produce hybrids. The stands of berries we find in the countryside today tend to be the products of these marriages. Take note that, without chemical sprays, fertilizers, or the attention of man, berry bushes produce loads of fruit in the wild, and they will do the same in your yard.

A hundred years ago, millions of pounds of berries were produced and sold at American markets. In those days, agricultural workers were still treated like slaves and paid just about as much. When it became necessary to treat people like human beings and the cost of labor went up, berries slowly started to disappear from the stores. So, too, did what was once common knowledge: the use of blackberries and raspberries as medicine.

Berry plants have figured in health maintenance and preservation for thousands of years. In Asia, the Korean raspberry is still used as a tonic to improve the health of someone suffering from chronic illness or general weakness. The berries are also made into jam and dried for use in medicinal teas. In Europe, the old-time herbalists recommended the berry for similar purposes as well as for diarrhea and fevers. The Native Americans used blackberries to strengthen the constitution and to build up gynecological health. In all three cultures, the berries were made into syrups taken every day to promote vim and vigor. The common belief is that components in the berries, roots, and leaves fire up the engines of life and stimulate health.

The raspberry is a trailing shrub, which means that its nature is to shoot its stems up in the air. Then, bowing to the pressure of gravity, these stems bend back down towards the ground where they put out new roots. The plant produces new stems, or canes as they are known, and these in turn produce the fruit we are so excited to eat. When you buy raspberry plants from a mail-order source, which is the way to go, you will be sent some stubs of canes that have been clipped down, with roots attached. From this stub-and-root combo will shoot the new fruit-bearing canes in the spring.

I mention getting your berry canes from mail-order sources because they have the best prices and the most varieties. Raspberries come in red, black, purple, and yellow, each with a slightly different flavor. You might want to plant a tutti-frutti assortment for the widest possible range of mouth experiences. Blackberries only come in one color, but they do have a considerable range of shapes and growing habits. Thorn-free blackberries are one of the best creations Luther Burbank ever dreamed up.

The stub you receive in the mail needs to be planted in a fairly sunny location and so that the roots are entirely covered with soil. Despite the fact that they like sun, raspberries will take a pretty high amount of shade, which makes them easy to grow in most sites. Once the stub is planted, you have only to keep it watered. In a matter of weeks, the new cane will shoot up, ready to blossom and bear fruit.

Like many of the plants in the no-care Flower Garden, raspberries and blackberries appreciate; each year more and more plants will spring from your original planting. Eventually, you will have to thin the plant and either throw out or give away the surplus canes.

GRAPES

The grapevine is fast growing enough for even the most impatient gardener. It's exactly the kind of dynamic, energetic plant that can make your garden a place you'll want to be. With no further ado, let me introduce you to the one plant you absolutely must possess.

The grape was one of the very first cultivated plants; early human beings seem to have discovered this wonder just about the time they made the transition from hunters and gatherers to settlement dwellers. It's hard to miss. A single vine can easily overtake a 150-foot tree, covering the entire frame with hundreds of pounds of fruit. Early man probably took one look at what the grape did all on its own and said, "Maybe I should include some of that in my garden plan."

Part of the reason people historically have been so enamored with the grapevine is its productivity—with only slight assistance, it will yield a tremendous amount of food. In the days when you either farmed or died, such plants were the subsistence farmer's best friend, and the ancient Egyptians, Israelites, Greeks, and Romans all considered the grapevine a symbol of fertility for reasons too obvious to mention.

The plant itself is said to be a native of Asia Minor, otherwise known as the cradle of civilization. It seems that as long as the grape has produced its fruit, man has pressed the fruit into wine. Thought of more as food than a beverage in the earliest days, wine was commercially produced in Assyria, Babylonia, Lydia, Syria, Israel, and Phoenicia hundreds of years before the Christian era.

The earliest wine was made by storing fresh grape juice in goatskin bags until it was fully fermented. One of the problems facing the ancients was food preservation. Most food was produced in the summertime, but as our forbearers had to eat year-round, they looked for ways to keep their produce edible beyond its natural moment of ripeness. They discovered that grape juice thus stored would remain potable indefinitely, and so they made a lot of wine to keep themselves fed in the winter months.

They discovered too that the grapes could be dried in the sun to produce raisins. The ancient Israelites also boiled grape juice down into a thick and gooey substance called "dibbs." As the sugar content of this crude sort of jelly was high enough to prevent spoiling, once again the grape became a major source of year-round food. Throughout the Old Testament, references are made to the fact that each man should possess his own grapevine, which is just what we are going to do.

Grapes are easy to grow, and they're guaranteed to produce so much fruit that you too will have to decide whether to make wine, raisins, or dibbs. In the garden, this is the right kind of problem to have; plants that overproduce are much more fun than those that just whimper along. The grapevine does not whimper.

To start growing grapes, all you have to do is run to the garden center, buy yourself a grapevine, and plant it according to the directions. Mother Nature will handle the rest. Grapevines do require a support on which to grow, however, and though you could train your vine to a tree, that makes harvesting the grapes rather difficult. I suggest that you train your grapevine to an arbor or trellis, as this will keep the grapes right where you need them, in hand's reach.

When you select your grapevine, ask the garden center personnel how seedless grapes do in your area. They do better in some climes than in others, but if you can grow seedless, you probably ought to do this—spitting all those seeds out is rather tedious. The old standard seeded grape is the concord, and this variety will do marvelously under all circumstances.

STRESS-ERCISES

• • • • • • • • • • • Preliminary Exercise • • • • • • • • • • •

Head out to the garden with your trusty lawn chair and take a seat. Tilt your head back and stare at the sky. Note its color and the birds flying overhead. See if you can watch the clouds move with the winds. Take about ten minutes to study the sky. After you have accomplished this exercise, do one of the following.

• • • • • • • • • • • ❦ *One* ❦ • • • • • • • • • • •

Get up from your chair and check the progress of your fruit plants and the fruit they are bearing. See how much the watermelons have grown, note the development of the berries, examine your apple tree. Do a survey of the fruit

An important part of any stress-relieving program is learning how to be nice to ourselves.

and imagine eating it when it becomes ripe. Visualize the finished product being dropped into your mouth.

············ ❦ *Two* ❦ ············

Sit under the grape arbor, pick some fruit, and eat it. Take the time to really savor the flavor, contemplating how wonderful fruit really can taste.

············ ❦ *Three* ❦ ············

When the fruit is in season and you have a surplus, sit on your chair with an old-fashioned recipe book. Go through the volume, find a recipe that appeals to you, pick the necessary fruit, and make something delicious. Invite friends over and share the experience.

MAIL-ORDER SUPPLIERS OF FRUIT-PRODUCING PLANTS:

AMES ORCHARD AND NURSERY
18292 Wildlife Road
Fayetteville, AR 72701
501-443-0282

EXOTICA RARE FRUIT NURSERY
P.O. Box 160
Vista, CA 92085
619-724-9093

FOWLER NURSERIES
525 Fowler Road
New Castle, CA 95658
916-645-8191

GURNEY'S SEED & NURSERY COMPANY
110 Capital Street
Yankton, SD 57079
605-665-1671

J. W. JUNG SEED COMPANY
335 South High Street
Randolph, WI 53957-0001
800-247-JUNG

NORTHWOODS RETAIL NURSERY
27635 S. Oglesby Road
Canby, OR 97013
503-266-5432

PACFIC TREE FARMS
4301 Lynwood Drive
Chula Vista, CA 91910
619-422-2400

RAINTREE NURSERY
391 Butts Road
Morton, WA 98356
206-496-6400

SOUTH MEADOW FRUIT GARDENS

15310 Red Arrow Highway

Lakeside, MI 49116

616-469-2865

STARK BROTHERS

P.O. Box 10

Louisiana, MO 63353-0010

800-325-4180

· · · · · · · · · · · · ❧ · · · · · · · · · · · · · ·

CHAPTER FIVE

The Vegetable Garden

When I was about 12 years old, my grandfather came to visit during summer vacation. By some twist of fate, when he left the District of Columbia to return to Richmond, I ended up in the car with him. This grandfather was my father's father, the one who helped me plant my first vegetable garden, and he shared a home with his sister, my Great-aunt Elizabeth.

They lived in a little white clapboard house with green shutters in a Richmond neighborhood long since past its prime. Both sides of the house were planted with gardenia bushes that erupted in a sickeningly sweet smell each August, the time of my visit. During the hot nights, the scent of gardenias would roll into the bedrooms like fog over London. Needless to say, this suburban, air-conditioned child just about died each night in the 100° swelter. I can remember lying on starched sheets, sweating like a pig, gagging at the ever-present fragrance of gardenia, wishing and praying for a cool breeze. The nights were a bit rough, but the days were lots of fun.

Aunt Elizabeth made the most marvelous dinners, most of which featured foods from my grandfather's vegetable garden. Fried chicken was the crown jewel of the dining table, surrounded by tomato-and-onion salad, green beans, creamed corn, kale greens, fried summer squash, and mashed potatoes. She had a way of putting together a simple yet delectable meal with effortless grace. Her dinners lacked the frills of fashionable cuisine, but they were loaded with a depth and spirit that fancy food will never have. Raised on a farm and taught to prepare meals for people who needed their strength, Aunt Elizabeth was a world-class cook in my estimation.

My grandfather and I would run around town doing this and that until about midday, when we would return to his home to help Elizabeth with dinner. He tended the vegetable garden, and she did the cooking. I sat on the porch, processing the produce my grandfather picked, shucking black-eyed peas and pulling the plugs out of the tomatoes. Collecting, preparing, and cooking dinner filled several hours and was a major feature of my stay. It took a lot of time, but these old southerners took that time. They were in no rush, especially in August.

My grandfather was no stranger to alcohol and smoked three packs of filterless cigarettes a day. Still, he lived well into his 80s, healthy as can be. When his time ran out, it wasn't that his body gave in—he fell on his head. I am convinced that he lived as long as he did because he didn't lead a stressful life. He took the time to plant the black-eyed peas, pick them, shuck them, and eat them. While he was doing all of the above, he did not worry that the world couldn't get on without his presence. The man lived by one of my favorite Chinese proverbs: "Always go to an emergency leisurely." Walter Schar wouldn't rush out of a burning house, and you know, he never got sick.

We are going to grow a garden my grandfather would have approved of and cook a meal Aunt Elizabeth would have cooked. In case you are interested, here's the menu:

... ⚘ ...

Tomato-and-onion salad

Green beans

Creamed corn

Kale greens

Fried summer squash

Mashed potatoes

Fried chicken

This is a two-part activity: first you have to grow the food, then you have to take the time to make the meal. In both phases, pretend you are living in Richmond and it's 103° out, and try to move the way a slug does. As I've said before, a big part of the stress problem is that we move too fast. Use this garden as an opportunity to slow down.

TOMATOES

We all know you can't get a decent tomato at the grocery store. Commercially grown tomatoes are pathetic, and as strange as it may seem, a lot of work has gone into making them this way. Scientists created the modern nightmare tomato in the lab, which is exactly where it looks as if it was grown. Some years back, plant-breeders saw the writing on the wall. Agricultural labor was becoming a problem, and mechanically harvested crops were the wave of the future. They developed a tomato that could be picked by a machine, hurled 30 feet into the air by another machine, and, here's the catch, still not bruise. Of course, the tomatoes had to be picked green and then gassed to achieve that marvelous pink coloration and total lack of flavor. So you see, commercial tomatoes are bad by design. There's no serendipity here.

Though the tomato is in a terrible state today, it has been hauled all over the world in the handbags of humanity because in its natural state, it's a gift from the gods. The Native Americans were using it as a food source centuries before white men first landed on American shores. The Aztec word for this

If your days ever seem to be treating you the way a tomato picker treats a tomato, you're reading the right book.

111

fruit is *tomatl*, which in time became *tomato*. The plant grows wild in the temperate climate of what we now call Latin America. There, hundreds of tomato varieties exist today, both in the garden and in the wild.

In the late 1500s, Cortez is credited with hauling it back from the New World to Spain, the tomato's first stop on the European tour. Arab traders picked up the tomato in Spain, took it to Morocco, and from there Italian sailors carried it to Italy. Tomatoes and Italian cooking seem one and the same today, so it's hard to imagine that until the 17th century, the Italians had never seen one. Clearly, once it arrived in Italy, it became quite popular. It was called *pomo dei moro*, or the "Moor's apple."

That name, *pomo dei moro*, was to cause the tomato all kinds of problems in other parts of Europe, where people misinterpreted it to mean *pomo d'amor*, or the "love apple." The Germans and English have always had a problem with sex, and surprise, surprise, the polite people from these societies wouldn't eat the fruit due to its name. The tomato was thought to be an aphrodisiac, heaven forbid.

Worse yet, the tomato is related to and resembles the deadly nightshade plant, which had long been associated with the devil and witchcraft. The Puritans got wind that eating a tomato might make you a little randy, and even before they left Europe for New England, they began mounting a vicious campaign against it. Witches and tomato growers received similar treatment under the Puritans. More than one member of the Puritan community got put out for daring to grow the "devil's fruit."

As if this early American fascism wasn't enough, the medical community got in on the ban-the-tomato wagon, stating in no uncertain terms that the tomato was deleterious to the health. The physicians felt that the tomato peel was indigestible and would stay in the stomach forever (sound like the bubble gum story?), causing cancer. Between the Puritans and the doctors, Americans kept clear of the tomato for a long time.

It was only when the Italians started pouring into the country with tomatoes in tow at the beginning of the 20th century that other European colonials warmed to it. After people saw the Italians eating tomatoes and living to tell the story, they followed suit. The tomato came into its own nationally with the introduction of a product known as catchup. "Catchup" is actually a Malaysian word referring to any number of sauces. Like chutney and mint jellies, catchup was served alongside meals as a condiment.

Dutch traders picked up the concept and brought it to Europe, from whence it traveled to America. The Heines company introduced a product, Heines 57 catchup, at the beginning of the 20th century. Though most catchups of the day were made of walnuts, Heines' new invention contained the very risque tomato. The product became the national rage, and housewives who wanted to make a homemade version thereof were forced to plant a few "love apples" in their backyards. In time, people discovered what the Native Americans already knew: the tomato was indeed fit for human consumption. Though the American story had a sad start, it has had a happy ending; the tomato is the number-one homegrown vegetable in the country. As the state of the store-bought varieties worsens, it may become an even more popular vegetable garden plant than it is today.

As far as raising tomatoes in your garden plot, this should not be hard. They are vigorous growers that rarely displease the gardener. I learned a tomato-growing trick from an old-timer in Memphis, Tennessee, when I was working there and have used it ever since. When you purchase your tomato plants (beefsteak is my favorite), buy yourself a 50-pound bag of manure for every two plants you intend to grow. Dig a hole the size of a watermelon and take out the soil. Mix 25 pounds of manure with the removed soil, chopping well. Then plant your tomato in this mound of soil so that just the top two leaves are above the ground. If you bury the stem this way, the plant will form additional roots which can then soak up all the nutrition in that manure and convert it into tomatoes.

ONIONS

The onion is one of the oldest vegetables still in cultivation. It's a member of a famous branch of the lily family which includes such greats as garlic, shallots, chives, and leeks. For the purpose of procreation, the onion plant forms a bulb where energy is stored to produce seed the following year. The leaves of the onion use the sun and the nutrients it gathers from the soil to create sugar, which it then stores in its roots. When we snatch an onion out of the garden, we are stealing a year's worth of the sun's energy

stored in the fragrant little bulb. The odoriferous bulb is thought to have originated in Central Asia though it now grows on every continent on the planet. The plant was a favorite in all of the ancient worlds. The word *onion* comes to us from the Latin *unio*, or "united." To understand this, you have to know a little about garlic. If you have ever pulled a garlic clove apart, you know that what appears to be one solid item is in fact a series of separate objects. Unlike its cousin the garlic, an onion is a series of united layers that lie one atop the next and cannot be pulled apart, hence the name. From the Latin came the French *oignon*, and finally the modern English "onion."

Believe it or not, onions were once the prime ingredient in cough syrups, and rightly so—they contain expectorants and natural antibiotics.

Though we mainly consider the onion a source of flavor, it has long been used as a source of health, especially for colds, flu, and virus. Until the turn of the last century, the most popular cough syrups were onion syrups; whole onions were chopped and cooked with water and then honey to create concoctions billed as being able to cut a cough or flu in half. Sounds a little nasty, but onions do help the body eliminate mucous, and they also ease the pain of an irritated respiratory tract. Onion cough syrups can still be had at your finer natural food stores. In the world of herbalism, onions are seen as being strengthening to the overall constitution. As this is just what rundown, stressed-out people need, you might want to replace that daily apple with a daily onion.

The early Egyptians fed their Israelite slaves a steady diet of onions and garlic to keep them strong enough to build the pyramids. The Egyptians also used the vegetable as a body-stuffer in the process of mummifying their dead.

Compounds contained in the plant are antibacterial and would have slowed the decay of the corpse.

Baskets of onions were unearthed in the brothels of Pompeii. Somehow onions and prostitutes went hand-in-hand in those days. I'm not sure why, and I don't know that I want to hear the answer. The first Olympians were fed two onions with every meal to get their bodies in the finest form for competition. Since the beginning of human history, it seems, the onion has been viewed as a health aid, and it does in fact contain anticancer and antibacterial chemicals.

During the Middle Ages in Europe, the onion was considered a low-budget food on account of the rather unpleasant odor it can give the breath. The nobility shunned the smelly root and died young; the commoners ate all they could grow and were long-lived. You tell me who had the last laugh on this deal.

The first onions as we know them came to America on the Mayflower—the Native Americans had their own wild varieties, which were sometimes called wild garlic. Considerably smaller than the European onion, which can be as large as an apple, the wild bulbs were highly prized as both food and medicine.

Through the centuries of cultivation, man helped to create hundreds of onion varieties—white, red, and yellow skinned; some mild, others strong. For our purposes, however, we will plant whatever sort we can find at the hardware store. The time to plant your onions is in the early spring, just as the ground is warming. Run to the hardware, feed, or garden store, and get yourself a pound or two of onion sets. Onion sets are essentially seedling onions that, when planted, will grow and develop into onions large enough for the table. While you are getting your onions, get some manure. You'll need lots of this earthy plant food to produce big, sweet onions: one 50-bag of manure for every 8 square feet in your onion-growing area.

Just pour the manure on the ground and chop it into the soil until it is well mixed. Then plant your onion sets four inches apart and four inches below the soil's surface. Keep the plants well watered, and as your tomatoes ripen, your full-sized onions will be ready to harvest.

Aunt Elizabeth's Tomato-and-Onion Salad

4 onions	¼ teaspoon black pepper
4 tomatoes	1 cup white vinegar
1 teaspoon salt	2 tablespoons olive oil
2 tablespoons sugar	½ cup water

Peel the onions and put them into a pot of boiling water for one minute. Remove them and slice thinly. Slice the tomatoes to a desired thickness. Combine the salt, sugar, pepper, vinegar, olive oil, and water. Toss the mixture with the tomatoes and onions and refrigerate for two hours. Before serving, add more sugar and salt to taste. I like my tomatoes and onions afloat, but if you prefer less liquid, cut the water and vinegar quantities by half.

GREEN BEANS

It may come as a surprise to you, but the green bean is a Native American food. Its ancestor is said to have originated in Peru and traveled from that point well into Canada thousands of years before the first Europeans arrived in America. In conversation with a person of Native American ancestry, I recently learned his people's traditional use for this vegetable. The Indians gathered green beans, strung them on a thread the way red peppers are strung, and set them out to dry in the sun. The dried green beans were then hung from the house rafters and pulled down and boiled with a bit of meat to create a winter vegetable dish. In the mountains of Tennessee, country folk call this dish "strap beans."

The Native Americans grew their beans in an intriguing manner that my Grandmother Schar also employed. They planted them alongside their corn so that the cornstalks could serve as trellises for the bean vines. This planting scheme provided a perfect protein source as well as a clever way of dealing with the beans' need for a trellis.

We are going to plant Kentucky wonder pole beans, available at just about any hardware store. It's a variety that has given me consistently fabulous results. Since we are going to be planting them with the corn, we won't get into planting instructions here—you can find those in the following section on corn. One thing to remember about green beans, though, is that the more you pick them, the more they produce. Once your beans start producing, it's best to pick them just about every third day so you don't end up with over-sized and ever-so-tough beans. If you don't pick constantly, they will stop producing prematurely.

Green Beans

1 pound green beans	Cream
4 strips bacon	Salt
1 small onion, chopped	Black pepper
Vegetable oil	

Clean green beans and steam them gently until they are cooked through, about 10 minutes. Fry the bacon until it is done. In another pan, sauté the onion in vegetable oil until golden brown. Then crumble the bacon into the onions, add the green beans, and slowly heat the combination until the beans are cooked to your liking. Season with cream, salt, and pepper to taste. This dish can be prepared in advance and reheated in the oven just before dinner.

SWEET CORN

Another Native American plant, corn has been used for such a long time that no one is quite sure where in the New World the plant first grew. Most of our domestic plants have wild relatives, but not corn. The wild corn plant is extinct; where it originated and what it was like are mysteries. What is known is that corn descended from a grassy plant somewhere in central Mexico. Corn as we know it today has been found in archeological sites dating back 5,000 years, and the plant is presumed to have been in existence some time before that. It is perhaps one of the greatest discoveries of the New World. Along with soybeans, corn feeds the world, both directly and indirectly, as fodder for the animals we eat.

The Spanish took the first corn to Europe in the early 1500s, and within 40 years, the plant could be found growing in Africa and Asia as well as throughout Europe. That's pretty remarkable if you remember that in those days travel was slow; central Mexico is still a long way from Peking by pack-horse.

The sugar that makes corn sweet converts to starch quickly, so the best-tasting ears are cooked right after they're picked.

This rapid spread was partly due to the fact that corn is so easy to grow and requires so little processing to render it edible. Unlike wheat, which has to be pulled from the chaff, ground, and then baked before being consumed, corn can simply be peeled off the cob and then boiled or popped. In fact, the current rage, popcorn, is as old as the hills. It was even served at the first Thanksgiving dinner, thanks to a local chief, Quadequina, who brought deerskin bags filled with the treat.

Corn had been cultivated in the Americas for centuries when the white man first landed here, and he was greeted by several hundred varieties, some for popping, some for grinding, and some for eating fresh. Today we have the same three categories— popping corn (though all corn will pop), corn for meal, and eating or sweet corn—as well as feed corn for animals. Sweet corn varies from its other relations in the high sugar content of its moist, juicy kernels. They are quite literally filled with sugar and taste as sweet as the name suggests. This is the variety we will plant and cook for our country supper.

One of the best reasons for growing your own sweet corn is that as soon as the ear is picked, its sugar starts converting to starch. This means that corn, to be at its most flavorful, needs to go from the stalk directly into the pot of boiling water. Picking your own corn is the only way of tasting just how sweet sweet corn can be!

When you go to the hardware store, you will find that there are several varieties of sweet corn available. Frankly, I can't tell the difference between them. At the very least, you will have to choose white or yellow, and I'm sure you will be thrilled with either one.

Your corn will need to be planted in two rows for pollination purposes. Till the ground thoroughly so it is loose and fluffy. We will be planting corn and beans together as I explained in the previous section on beans. Both have hearty appetites, so I add a handful of manure with every seed I plant. Plant a bean seed with a corn seed every six inches in each row and water them well.

Creamed Corn

10 ears corn	2 tablespoons sugar
1 cup milk	Salt
1 tablespoon butter	2 tablespoons flour

Cut the kernels from the corn cobs with a sharp knife. Put them in a cast-iron skillet with half a cup of water and cook the corn until tender. Then add ¾ cup milk, butter, sugar, and salt, and stir until thoroughly blended. Use the remaining ¼ cup milk to dissolve the flour, then add to the skillet and mix well. Always taste as you go along and adjust with salt and sugar as you see fit.

KALE

Southerners are famous for their greens, be they kale, collard, mustard, land cress, dandelion, or poke, and no meal is considered complete without a sampling of several different kinds. These foods entered the American diet not from Indian sources, though many are native American plants, but rather from Africa. Like yams, peanuts, sesame seeds, and okra, kale was brought here by African slaves. Little has changed in its preparation since then. Contemporary Americans cook kale greens the same way they are cooked in Africa. In fact, Africans boil and chop their kale into a green mush almost identical to the one Aunt Elizabeth used to serve at her fried chicken dinners.

Kale is one of the oldest vegetable plants still cultivated today. Thought to be native to central Africa, it is now grown all over the world. The old slaves on the plantations believed that eating kale would improve the health, and they were right. No vegetable is more heavily laden with vitamins; kale also comes packed with all the anticancer chemicals that are characteristic of its fellow members of the cabbage family. A classic treatment for anemia, kale has an incredibly high iron content, making it just what the doctor ordered for a person suffering from what Aunt Elizabeth would call "tired poor blood." The water in which kale is first cooked is known as "pot liquor." It was traditionally given to those who were ailing and to pregnant women. This "liquor" tends to be black in color due to the vegetable's mineral content and very unpleasant in flavor. It's nothing you would want to enjoy over ice, but it's certainly chock-full of nourishment.

Essentially a headless cabbage, kale is one of the easiest greens to grow. Simply plant it in a bed in the early spring according to the instructions on the seed packet, and in a matter of four to six weeks, the kale will be large enough for picking. Pick the leaves individually—never pull the whole plant out—and it will continue producing well into the winter.

Kale Greens

1 pound kale	Salt
1 onion, chopped	Tabasco sauce
Vegetable oil	

Put the kale in a big pot and cover half-way with water. Bring the water to a boil, mash the kale around in it for two to three minutes, then strain it in a colander. In the same pot, sauté the onion in vegetable oil. When the onion is golden, add the kale back to the pot and simmer a few more minutes. Add salt and Tabasco to taste and cook over low heat for ten minutes.

SUMMER SQUASH

Good Aunt Elizabeth always fried summer squash—the yellow variety, of course—with onions and a touch of salt and pepper. (I didn't say stir-fried, I said fried.) The black pepper is a European addition, but the rest of the recipe is straight from the Native Americans' kitchen. The Indians fried it with bear fat, the colonials fried it with bacon fat, we fry it with vegetable fat, but the idea is basically the same. Scientists believe that these delicious plants

Zucchini bread, zucchini soup, zucchini lasagna, zucchini you-name-it: productivity is the reason for so many recipes.

were probably first grown not for their flesh but rather for their protein-filled seeds. As with the bean, traces of squash seeds have been found dating back 9,000 years.

The only problem with growing summer squash is that the plant is a producing fool. Each plant is capable of yielding anywhere between 30 and 70 pounds of squash. That's a lot of squash for one person to eat her way through, and most people who plant them can't bear the idea of eating one more ounce of squash by the end of the summer. This, of course, is the kind of problem we wouldn't mind having: a vegetable garden that overproduces.

With the squash plant's incredible productivity, there's no wonder that the plant spread from its native Columbian setting all the way to what we now call Chile and northward to Canada thousands of years before Europeans arrived in the Americas. The Native Americans were masters of easy agriculture, and they truly appreciated this plant. We Westerners tend to be overly involved with growing plants that don't really want to be grown, which is the equivalent of, shall we say, pushing organic fertilizer up a dry creek. We plant apples in dry locations when they want wet ones and oranges in states that aren't really warm enough to support them. The Indians had a different approach. They planted plants that flourished no matter what and that produced with the least amount of interaction or care. Suffice it to say that if they had the choice between spraying apples or collecting raspberries from the woods, they would have stuck with the raspberries. As modern gardeners on a time budget, we need to follow the Native American lead and stick with the sure bets.

The Native Americans were kind enough to pass along to the colonials their recipes for the vegetable which they called *askutasquash*. At that time, there were several thousand varieties of squash. Though every village and tribe had its own squashes, these usually fell into two categories—storage squashes and nonstorage squashes. Pumpkins and acorn squash are examples of storage squashes, which will stay good up to a year when stored in a dry location. Zucchinis and summer squash are good examples of nonstorage squashes. They must be eaten immediately, or they rapidly turn to mush.

Like the melons from the previous chapter on the Fruit Garden, summer squash needs to be planted in mounds, with three or four seeds to a mound. The best way to accomplish this is to take a 50-pound bag of manure and mix it with garden soil until you can't see any more distinct manure in the mound. Then just stick the seeds in the mound and wait. Before you know it, you will have enough squash for you and all your friends and relatives, too.

Fried Summer Squash

5 onions	Salt
10 summer squash	Black pepper
Vegetable oil	

The key to this operation is correctly frying the onions. Slice them and sauté them in vegetable oil until they are translucent and just a little brown on the edges. Then slice the summer squash in rounds and add it to the skillet. Stir constantly until the squash is cooked, which is a very subjective affair. I like mine well cooked; others like theirs more crispy. Salt and pepper to taste, and cover the dish until serving time.

POTATOES

Although the Irish are most usually associated with the potato, they actually got acquainted with the root vegetable rather late in the game. Potatoes are native to Central and South America and came to Ireland via Spain and the conquistadors. Ironically, potatoes made their way into the North American diet not from Central America, but rather from Europe and the English colonials. You could say that the potato is one of the first Americans to make a round trip to the Continent.

A relative of the tomato and the green pepper, the potato was a staple of the pre-Columbian diet. The Incas dried the tuber for year-round eating. They had thousands of names for what we now call the spud and just about as many varieties. The purple potato making inroads on the gourmet scene today represents just one of the hundreds of potato colors found in South America, ranging from black to white with every shade and tone in between.

My favorite potato story comes from the court of Queen Elizabeth I. It seems that she had gotten her hands on some spuds from a European source and had her kitchen garden staff plant them straight-away. However, upon harvesting the vegetable, the ignorant cooks tossed out the lumps at the ends of the roots and cooked up the greens. In case you didn't know it, potato greens are poisonous, and it seems that the meal moved all in attendance a little too close to their Maker for comfort. Word traveled, and the plant was banned from the royal table for a long time. In fact, even the common people were initially a little hesitant to eat the potato, and one monarch, Emperor Frederick Wilhelm, ordered his peasants to plant it or have their ears and noses chopped off. People eventually figured out what part was for eating and what part was for tossing out, and the potato became popular. Like corn, potatoes are easy to grow and easy to render edible.

When you eat a potato, what you are really eating is a swollen underground stem. Plants are largely interested in perpetuating themselves, and in this vein the potato plant takes the nutrition in the soil and mixes it with energy trapped from the sun to create sugar. This sugar then acts as the plant's food. When there is surplus, the potato takes the sugar, which is unstable and easily rots, and turns it into starch. The starch is then shipped down to the roots, which swell and in time form the hard balls we call potatoes. The potato plant is a masterful energy-trapper, and planting a few spuds will pay back high dividends.

You can buy potato sets at the garden center, but I never bother. Just purchase some good-sized potatoes at the grocery store and let them sit in the sun until they have sprouted eyes that are approximately one inch tall. Cut these potatoes into four pieces, each with a healthy clump of eyes firmly attached. Then plant the pieces about a foot apart in well-tilled and manured soil. The eyes will sprout into potato plants. When the greenery fades to brown, it's time to dig for your potatoes. This is a truly fun moment. The more you dig, the more potatoes you will find.

Now as to making mashed potatoes, I think we all know how to do that, but just in case, here's the recipe.

Mashed Potatoes

Potatoes	Salt
Milk	Black pepper
1 tablespoon butter	

Peel the potatoes and drop them in a pot of boiling water. Boil until the potatoes are cooked through, then drain them and mash them with a big spoon, adding milk, butter, salt, and pepper to taste.

Of course, we have yet to discuss the central attraction of this meal, the fried chicken. You may be looking at the menu and thinking it's hardly a health-food diet, but I must tell you that Aunt Elizabeth lived well into her late 80s and was fast on her feet the entire time. Her siblings ate the same diet and fared just as well. To my Aunt Elizabeth, this *was* health food, and her health certainly was good.

Fried Chicken

1 chicken	Vegetable oil
1 cup plus 2 tablespoons flour	4 garlic cloves
Salt	Tabasco sauce
Black pepper	1 can chicken stock
Cayenne pepper	

Cut up the chicken and place the pieces in a bowl of salted water for ten minutes to draw any excess blood. Remove the chicken from the bowl, dry it, and dump it into a brown paper bag. Add to this bag one cup of flour, salt, black pepper, and cayenne, and shake it vigorously. Heat a half-inch of vegetable oil in a cast-iron skillet. Put the floured chicken into the hot oil and season it with a little more salt and pepper, a touch of Tabasco, and four sliced garlic cloves. Fry the chicken until it is brown on both sides. Put the chicken on a plate and place it in the oven to keep it warm till dinner time. Pour the oil off the skillet, taking care to save all the accumulated drippings. Add ¾ can of chicken stock to them and bring the mixture to a boil. Use remaining ¼ can of chicken stock to dissolve two tablespoons of flour; add to mixture and stir constantly. Salt and pepper to taste. You can't have a country chicken dinner without chicken gravy, regardless of your cholesterol count.

STRESS-ERCISES

············ ❦ *One* ❦ ············

I said earlier that this was a two-part activity, but it's really a three-parter. After you've raised and cooked the food, you get to eat it. To maximize the stress loss, take an entire Sunday to harvest the vegetables and prepare the meal. Invite your best friends for dinner. As you sit down at the table, take a good look at all the food and think about the fact that you grew it yourself. As you

Imagine sitting down to a meal you produced with your own two little formerly stressed-out hands. This is getting back to basics in the very best way.

eat, take slow and deliberate bites, savoring the flavors. Repeat this exercise every weekend until the garden stops producing.

.... *Two* ....

Take a knife and a salt shaker out to your garden, pull a ripe tomato off the vine, cut it in half, hit it with a little salt, and bite into it. Treat yourself to a vegetable snack while relaxing in your chair.

MAIL-ORDER SUPPLIERS OF VEGETABLES:

W. ATLEE BURPEE COMPANY
300 Park Avenue
Warminster, PA 18974
215-674-4900

HENRY FIELD'S SEED AND NURSERY
415 North Burnett
Shenandoah, IA 51602
605-665-9391

GURNEY'S SEED & NURSERY COMPANY
110 Capital Street
Yankton, SD 57079
605-665-1671

BOOKS:

If you think that you would like to learn more about vegetable gardening, I have two fabulous books to recommend. The first is entitled *Blue Corn and Square Tomatoes* by Rebecca Rupp. Much of the background information about the vegetables in this chapter was gleaned from Ms. Rupp's entertaining work. The second is *The Self-Sufficient Gardener* by John Seymour. In my estimation, it is the best how-to-vegetable-garden book on the market. Easy to read, informative, and interesting from cover to cover, it will remain a consummate guide in all your gardening endeavors.

BLUE CORN AND
SQUARE TOMATOES
Rebecca Rupp
A Garden Way Publishing Book
Storey Communication, Inc.

THE SELF-SUFICIENT GARDENER
John Seymour
Dolphin Books
Doubleday and Company, Inc.

CHAPTER SIX

· · · · · · · · · · · ❦ · · · · · · · · · · · · ·

The Water Garden

Several years ago, I went to Israel to visit a childhood friend who lived on a kibbutz a few hours from Tel Aviv. The bus ride was long, and it was followed by what seemed like an extra long walk from the bus stop to the kibbutz itself. There's nothing like wandering around in a war-torn country without a clue where you are going to stir up a little stress. By the time I got to the commune's gates, I was hot, tired, and ready to scream. I felt myself on the edge of a real fit, and believe me, when I go off, people take to the bomb shelter.

When I finally found my friend in the maze of identical housing (everyone is equal on a kibbutz, and everybody's house looks just the same), he must have sensed my foul humor because he immediately took me for a walk. It was sunset, and we strolled down to the lake where we sat and caught up with each other's news. I was still feeling testy when we sat down, but surprisingly, my anxiety slowly faded as I watched the water gently break on the shore and the water birds fly around. The sun seemed to drop right into the

It's okay to talk to your fish. If they talk back, seek professional help.

lake so that I halfway expected to see hot vapor shooting up at the horizon line. All the tension drained out of my body, and in short order I was restored to some semblance of sanity. There was such a deep sense of calm about that lake that I can recall it to this day.

The truth of the matter is that when you spend some time interacting with water, you trade your mental chaos in for peace and serenity. It doesn't seem to make a shred of sense, now does it? But scientists have proven that hanging out with water impacts the mind and body for the better. How it does this is still a mystery. And it can remain one as far as we're concerned; let's just remember to take advantage of the facts.

Water exercises a calming effect. A walk on a beach, a stroll along a lake, or a float down a river all result in a person's feeling serene. Ocean-front property is globally valued for this very reason: water's ability to settle the nerves, or, to put it in the context of this book, to remove the stress from our systems. If you live anywhere near a highway that services the beach routes, you know what people will go through to get to the ocean.

Imagine resting on a deserted beach, standing on the rocky bank of a fast-moving river, or dropping pebbles into a still pond and watching the ripples radiate out. Shut your eyes and visualize the scenes. This activity alone can slow the mind down. As with the rest of our stress-relieving theme gardens, our next garden harnesses the power of nature to our advantage. In this case, it's the power of water.

We are going to create a private water scene where you can spend time each day, dumping your stress and having the void you've just created there filled with peace. Unlike the tranquilizers people use to achieve the same end, with this form of self-medication, there are no side effects beyond the occasional mosquito bite.

A number of cultures don't suffer at the murderous hands of stress the way we do. People in these societies have similar lives and work schedules, and they face the same kinds of life changes we face. Yet they don't get all the stress-related illnesses we do. It seems they have means of dumping their stress so that it doesn't eat away at them. The facts indicate that they are doing something we aren't, something that we had better start doing real soon. The key lies in maintaining an active relationship with nature.

The Japanese have a high gross national product, but by American standards, they have a low incidence of stress-related illnesses. The Japanese are famous for taking the time to travel to Kyoto to experience the cherry blossoms. They board buses and head to the hills at the crack of spring to collect mountain vegetables. They journey to places where they can commune with nature as often as they can. They also garden in a big way. One of the more common gardening techniques employed by the Japanese is water gardening.

The Japanese have found that connecting with nature infuses a person with vital energy, which is just what we need to get through the hectic and maddening game that is modern life. As they cannot go tripping off to the mountains, the sea, or the lake on a daily basis, they instead create in their gardens perfect examples of nature. A tiny urban backyard is designed to look like a bamboo forest; a mid-sized backyard is designed to look like a series of lakes with interconnecting streams. One of my favorite Japanese gardens is a tiny backyard converted to look like a forest. Imagine that you could come home from work each evening and sit in the middle of a forest. You'd certainly be more relaxed there than you would be inside watching the nightly death-and-destruction report, otherwise known as the news.

The Japanese use their gardens to create nature refuges for themselves, and because they do, they are especially attuned to the value of adding water to the scene. Let's just say that the Japanese have developed water gardening to a fine art. In Japan, the practice is several thousand years old and filled with history and tradition. Whereas we might add a few goldfish to our water gardens, the Japanese add the highly esteemed koi carp to theirs. One of the better koi carp can cost upwards of $500,000. That's taking your water gardening seriously!

The Japanese go to such extremes with their water gardens because they have discovered that having water in one's outdoor space is a boon to the mental health. Having his own private lake offers the gardener the opportunity to run outside and get a dose of peace whenever he needs it. It's an intensely practical endeavor. Whatever energy a water garden requires to install and maintain is a small price to pay for what it gives back to you in mental well-being. You know the saying, a mind is a terrible thing to waste. Well, that's especially true when it's yours.

The object of a Japanese water garden is to provide a setting where the gardener can relax and meditate. The aim is to create a scene so visually captivating that a person simply forgets all else and easily enters a quiet and peaceful frame of mind.

This idea of meditation is a tricky one for many of us Westerners because we don't know a whole lot about it. In simplest terms, meditation is a means of taking a person from an irritated and mentally chaotic state of mind to a serene and quiet state of mind. If on one side of the spectrum, you have whirling thoughts and on the other you have peace, then meditation is the bus you are going to ride to get from one side to the other.

So how do you board this bus? Install a water garden. There is an old European fable about a king who was going out of his mind with boredom. He was so agitated about it that he offered his daughter's hand in marriage to any magician who could make time fly. The magicians came and went, none able to accomplish the task. Needless to say, the king was becoming more and more vile with the departure of each. Finally, a magician showed up and boldly announced that he could make time fly. He told the king to put on his walking shoes, and off the two went into the countryside. The magician took the king to a stream and instructed him to take off his shoes and to wade in the water. Once the king was barefoot and sloshing around, the magician said, "Let's try to catch a frog." So the two jumped about, turning rocks over, chasing frogs here and there, and when the king looked up, he saw that the sun was setting. Time had flown. The point of this tale is as follows: playing is meditating, and a water garden is an ideal setting for some play.

By now you are probably thinking, this sounds like a ton of work, and I am not interested in having a huge hole dug in my yard. There was a day when water gardens were quite difficult to install, but that's not the case any more. Converting a traditional garden space into a wonderful water garden bound to relax even the most uptight in our ranks is easier than you would think.

On the most basic level, all that is required to set up a water garden is a water-tight container. If you talk to the folks who sell water-gardening supplies, they will attempt to complicate this matter substantially. This makes sense—the more complicated they make it, the more products you have to buy. But believe you me, all that is required to water garden is an item that will hold the water.

I have seen people use buckets, washtubs, bathtubs, whiskey barrels cut in half—you name it. There are as many possibilities out there as there are days in the year. One of the more popular techniques of late is to dig a hole and line it with a water-garden liner, which is essentially a watertight rubber sheet. This is a good option but a costly one. For our purposes, we are going to keep things as easy as is humanly possible and as cheap. If you want to explore other alternatives, any one of the several concerns selling water-gardening supplies will be more than happy to oblige.

In this Water Garden, we are going to use a regulation horse trough, available at any feed store for a fraction of the expense and trouble of digging a hole and lining it with either concrete or a rubber liner. Horse troughs are cheap and easy to work with. Should you grow tired of the water garden, all you have to do is drain the trough and put it out with the trash.

Step One: Selecting the trough

These troughs come in a variety of shapes and sizes, some long and narrow and others short and fat. You can select whatever size works best with your space, but we are going to use a six-foot-long trough. These are about 2½ feet wide.

Step Two: Refinishing the trough

Though the horse trough is intensely practical for our beginning water-gardening purposes, it is not one of the more attractive features. Its basic sheet-metal tone is no gift to our Garden of Eden, and so our next step is to paint the outside of the trough a more palatable color. In this case, we are going to paint it grey with white-and-black splatter marks. You can paint your trough however you like; it might be fun to check out some of the faux finish books if you are interested in, say, having one that looks like marble. After you paint the trough, go over the paint with one coat of polyurethane to make it last longer.

Step Three: Partially submerging the trough

The trough stands almost three feet tall, and for aesthetic purposes we will sink it down into the ground one foot. Upon placing the trough, draw its shape on the ground and dig a similarly shaped hole one foot deep. Place the trough in the hole and smooth the removed soil around its sides.

Step Four: Adding the sump pump water fountain

A water fountain is included in the trough for several reasons, both aesthetic and practical. Nothing could be nicer than the sound of a fountain. Also, the movement of the water adds oxygen, which our little fishy friends need to sustain life. You can purchase a basic sump pump at the hardware store, but you will need to have access to an electric current to run it, so bear this in mind as you site your water garden. Drill a hole large enough to pass the plug through the top of the trough. This will help you hide the electronics. You can attach a simple pipe to the sump pump to create a fountain, or you can hook it to a real fountain feature. Water garden mail-order companies offer many fountains, but be forewarned that they can be pricey.

Step Five: Adding water

With all the previous steps accomplished, you can add your water. Stick the hose in the trough and let her rip. Remember, though, that it's best to let water sit and "soften" for a week before adding plants and fish. This allows the chlorine that exists in most of our water supplies to evaporate, leaving the water more hospitable to vegetable and animal life.

Step Six: Adding water plants

There are two kind of water plants, those that live under the water and those that live above it. We are going to be planting water lilies and water iris above and anacharis under the waves. As for the water lilies and water iris, you can either buy them at the local water-gardening supply store or ask a friend for a cutting. Both grow rapidly, and someone with a water garden should be more than happy to share a piece of the constantly multiplying supply. They tend to be rather expensive at the store, so getting a cutting for free is a much preferable option.

Though these two plants grow in water, their roots grow in soil, so they have to be planted in pots. If you buy the water plants, they will come potted, and you won't have to fuss with the pots. To pot your own cutting, simply fill a five-gallon terra cotta pot with garden soil and stick the cutting in the middle of the pot. The plant will take care of the rest.

The water lily pot can be dropped into the trough and allowed to sink to the bottom. The plant's leaves will grow to reach the water's surface. The water iris pot needs to rest on a concrete block, as these plants naturally grow just six inches below the surface. The anacharis, a common aquarium plant, can be purchased at any pet store and simply dropped into the trough as is—it requires no soil to grow.

Step Seven: Adding fish

Though the Japanese buy expensive fish, we will settle for a dozen of the so-called feeders available at pet stores. These baby goldfish are destined for the mouths of snakes and carnivorous fish, and by buying them and giving them a home, you are incurring a karma bonus. Beyond this, they are really cheap, and until your water garden ages a bit, it doesn't pay to put expensive fish in it. Don't be surprised if you lose half of the 12. Some will survive, and six is just about the right number of fish for this size water garden. Buy some cheap goldfish food while you are at the pet store. For your purposes, you do not need one of the designer brands.

A word of caution. There are a lot of scalpers involved with this fish business, and they will try to sell you a bunch of high-priced fish and unnecessary fish supplies. More than one pet store owner, attempting to steer me towards a more expensive purchase, has told me that feeder goldfish wouldn't live in a pond setting. The fact is that several of my "doomed" feeders

While most of us know how soothing a walk along the ocean or a lake shore can be, water gardening and the peace it affords still seem to be a well-kept secret.

have gone on to become beautiful 14-inch fish. Later you may choose to explore some of the more expensive options in both food and fish, but for now stick with the feeders.

The feeders will be sold in a plastic, water-filled bag. Take them in their bag out to the water garden and let it float for 20 minutes before releasing them. This allows the fish time to adjust to the water temperature, minimizing the shock of their change in environment. Feed the fish once a day, ringing a little bell before you feed. Doing this will train the fish to come to the surface of the water at the sound of the bell.

Step Eight: Landscaping the trough

When the water garden is up and running, it's time to do some landscaping to integrate it into its surroundings. As the Japanese would tell us, all things in the garden must work together to create a whole, and at present we just have a pool of water standing out in the middle of nowhere. To create a more natural feeling to the overall water garden, add the following items: one Korean birch tree, three azaleas, and ten fern plants. Actually, these plants are suggestions that happen to be my own favorites—a trip to your garden center will result in your finding just the plants that will look nice around your pool.

Once you have installed your water garden, your biggest problem will be hauling yourself out there for your energy boost. The key to losing your stress is regular involvement with nature, with an emphasis on the word *regular*. This is the reason I included the fish in the water garden. Unless you are prepared to see your finny friends go belly up, you will want to get out there and feed them on a regular basis. It's a trick, I know, but it works.

STRESS-ERCISES

• • • • • • • • • • • Preliminary Exercise • • • • • • • • • • • •

Head out to your chair, which should be squarely located next to your water garden. Sit down, close your eyes, and spend ten minutes really listening to the sounds of the fountain splashing water. Do some deep-breathing exercises while you're at it. Then proceed to one of the following exercises.

············ ❧ *One* ❧ ············

Feed the fish and watch them eat. You will have to stand back and be as quiet as possible, otherwise you will scare them off. Try to get to know their individual personalities.

············ ❧ *Two* ❧ ············

Close your eyes and smell the scent of the water lily bloom.

············ ❧ *Three* ❧ ············

Feed the fish. Then close your eyes and listen to the sounds of their bobbing up to grab some of that food.

············ ❧ *Four* ❧ ············

Go out in a rain storm and watch the rain hitting the surface of your mini-lake. Close your eyes and listen to the sounds it makes.

············ ❧ *Five* ❧ ············

Sit in your chair and examine the pool, part by part. Look at the water lily leaves and the way they float on the surface. Notice how the occasional insect inadvertently lands in the water, how the fish come up to the surface from time to time.

MAIL-ORDER SUPPLIERS OF WATER-GARDENING EQUIPMENT:

MARYLAND AQUATIC NURSERY INC.
3427 N. Furnacc Road
Jarrettsville, MD 21084
410-557-7615

PARADISE WATER GARDENS
14 May Street
Whitman, MA 02382
617-447-4711

PERRY'S WATER GARDENS
191 Leatherman Gap Road
Franklin, NC 28734
704-524-3264

········· ❧ ···········

CHAPTER SEVEN

The Compost Pile

At last we come to the title garden, the Compost Pile. We are going to explore the wild world of organic matter in the process of returning to the earth. It's not what most people think of when they hear the word "garden," but the compost pile is a garden nevertheless, and an indispensable, dynamic one at that.

In its simplest terms, composting is taking organic material and allowing it to break down into what is called compost, a rich black substance that the gardener—that's you—will use to mulch plants. What goes into the compost pile? Anything organic. More specifically, grass clippings, raked leaves, weeds pulled from the garden, potato peelings, the wilted outer leaves of lettuce, and so on. Any plant material can be placed in the compost pile.

The site where composting takes place is traditionally called the compost pile. When you keep dumping organic material in the same spot, before you know it, you will have a pile. Once the material is in this pile, insects, bacteria, and fungus of all sorts will feed on it and reduce it to mulch. You can continue to dump organic material on the pile, or you can build a box with chicken wire or boards to contain it. Some like the open-air look, others the tidier, boxed version. Either way, your organic contributions will decompose into compost. This soil-like substance is your plants' best friend, and they will repay you well for providing it.

You may be asking yourself why you should bother with this activity. It's a valid question. To understand the importance of composting, you first need to understand a bit about the interaction between plants and soil. To you, soil may just be the brown stuff that sits outside your door and turns into mud when it's mixed with water. Soil, however, is much more than mere dirt. It's like a living creature, and it needs nourishment just as all creatures do. Soil is actually a multi-faceted organism in which millions of actors and reactors all coexist.

Worms, grubs, fungus, bacteria, and all forms of microbes live in soil. At first, this may sound rather repulsive because we are generally taught that bacteria, bugs, and fungus are bad things to be killed at every turn. This entirely untrue notion must be tossed out the window and onto the compost pile right way. The bacteria, bugs, and fungus in the soil keep it healthy. Yes, there are some bad or pathogenic soil-dwellers, but generally the good players keep the bad ones in line and under control. Remember that nature works just fine. It has worked for millions of years, and it will continue to do so if we let it be.

Soil is really a living mat, a complex apartment house, if you will, with lots of different tenants. Each has a job to do. Plants send their roots down into the soil and pull up from it all the essential elements they need to sustain life. They are a part of the ecosystem of the soil, and if the soil isn't healthy, the plants will not be healthy. Adding compost to the soil around your plants stimulates the health of the soil and thereby stimulates the health of the plants. The compost is rich food for all the many creatures that live in the soil. It

Peeling potatoes is a relaxing job; it forces you to slow down to a reasonable human pace. And carrying the peels to the compost pile gives you the chance to slow down even further, to nature's pace.

pays to feed them because they are the keepers of the soil, and you want them to be able to do their job.

Composting couldn't be simpler; you are merely aligning yourself with the forces of nature. If you have ever walked in the woods, you will have noticed the layers of leaves on the forest floor. Many of the leaves in the uppermost layer are still whole, but as you dig deeper, you see that in successive layers the leaves have broken down and formed a rich, soil-like substance. This process of decay and return to the soil is one of the most basic principles on the planet. As soon as things stop living, the forces of nature—bacteria, insects, and so forth—work together to return them to soil.

There are many different approaches to composting, but the bottom line is that whichever way you do it, when you put organic material in a pile, it will return to soil. The particulars of how you stack your organic material do not matter—nature will take its course.

In case you are wondering, compost does not smell, and it doesn't attract vermin. These are the two excuses people always spout when discussing why they don't have a compost pile. Nature works silently and effortlessly, and in this case, without producing any odors. Animal wastes are the items that tend to stink, and we won't be adding any of them to the compost pile.

The key to successful composting is religiously putting all organic material with which you come into contact onto the compost pile, be it leaves or the brown outer shell of an onion. If you do so, you will eventually have a rich supply of compost. The process takes a while, so from the time you start, you are looking at about a year before you can harvest your first compost. To do so, just dig the compost from the bottom of the pile and place it around your plants or hoe it in a bit. Always add some compost when planting seeds or cuttings. Use it liberally here, there, and everywhere.

STRESS-ERCISES

············ ❧ *One* ❧ ············

Keep a bucket in the kitchen and fill it with all your produce waste: potato peelings, carrot scrapings and ends, wilted lettuce, and so forth. Never, ever, throw organic waste out or put it down the disposal. Every night after dinner, take the bucket out to the compost pile, dig a hole in the pile, and bury the contents of the bucket. You can dump it on top, but shoveling speeds the decomposition process.

·············· ❧ *Two* ❧ ··············

Toss all weeds, grass clippings, and fallen leaves on top of the pile. Go out to the garden and scavenge for pieces of plant material for the compost. When your neighbors put their leaves out for trash collection, add them, too.

·············· ❧ *Three* ❧ ··············

Every once in a while, water your compost pile. Adding water speeds the composting process, as all the micro-critters in the compost need lots of moisture to do their work. Spend a few minutes watering the pile and listening to the sounds it creates. More than one compost pile has been known to gurgle.

·············· ❧ *Four* ❧ ··············

After putting a big load of material such as grass clippings or raked leaves on the compost pile, water it well for four days. Once the compost has had a few days to get working, dig into it with a shovel and watch the steam pour out.

·············· ❧ *Five* ❧ ··············

Once a week write all your troubles on a tiny piece of paper. Wad this piece of paper up into a ball, take the ball out to the compost pile, and bury it. As you do, tell Mother Nature that you can't deal with these problems and you know that she can. Leave them with her. If they continue to dominate your thoughts, repeat the exercise as often as necessary.

·············· ❧ *Six* ❧ ··············

Go out to the compost pile, lift some compost up with a shovel, and have yourself a good smell. The fragrance won't be unpleasant—more like a deep, earthy scent—but I wouldn't suggest that you use your deep-breathing exercises in this particular aromatherapy go-round.

COMPOSTING PART TWO: THE CHICKEN GARDEN

If you enjoyed the section on composting, you are really going to get a kick out of this one. Many garden features build on each other, and this is literally the case with my next suggestion. You can leave well enough alone and stay with the compost pile, or you can go one step further and add a few chickens to the equation.

Chickens have really gotten a bum rap in recent years, and they're frequently said to be stupid. As a chicken owner, I take offense at this observation, mostly because it generally comes from people who have never owned a chicken. Chickens are actually quite bright. Having had several, I can testify that they are in some ways smarter than a few people I know. What's more, they're a real asset to any garden, particularly those belonging to stressed-out gardeners.

At the turn of this century, there lived a brilliant woman by the name of Lady Balfour. Let's just say that she had a vision of the future, and she didn't like it one bit. She feared that humanity was going to abandon natural organic fertilizers for chemical ones. Since the beginning of time, human beings had collected the waste products of animals and added them to the soil to improve productivity. In Lady Balfour's day, people were starting to forsake natural fertilizers for factory-produced chemicals, and this didn't sit well with her.

We are now discovering what chemical fertilizers do to the earth: they ruin it. Unlike natural fertilizers that add to the health of the soil, chemical fertilizers disturb the balance that keeps the planet going. Lady Balfour developed a technique that allows people, regardless of how much or how little land they have, to produce their own natural organic fertilizer. Enter the chicken.

You might be asking yourself, why do we need a chicken when we already have a compost pile? The answer lies in the needs of the plants that we grow. The compost pile provides nutrition for both soil and plants, but it is missing one salient element crucial for the plants' growth, and that's nitrogen.

The three basic elements a plant needs to remain healthy are potash, phosphorous, and nitrogen. If you look on the back of most fertilizers, you will notice a formula, 1-1-1 or 2-5-8, for example. These formulas refer to the specific combination of potash, nitrogen, and phosphorus in the fertilizer. The

Man's best friend: the chicken. Add a hen or two to your compost heap, and you'll never have to buy fertilizer or eggs again.

nitrogen assists the plant in making stems and leaves to produce the sugars it needs to maintain itself. Phosphorus helps plants to reach maturity and produce flowers and seeds. The plant uses the potash in the growth process without which the plant can't survive.

By composting, you can provide your plants with all the potash and phosphorus they need, but no nitrogen. To create a complete plant food, you have to come up with a source for the third element. Lady Balfour had a solution to this problem. She recommended that one build a cage over the compost pile and add two chickens. The chickens' waste material (that's polite for feces) is loaded with nitrogen. Having chickens scratching around the compost leads to a balanced fertilizer, rich in all the elements plants need for strong growth. Not only do the chickens add the needed nitrogen, but they also speed the composting process by their incessant scratching. Two chickens on your compost pile will reduce its processing time down from one year to two months. That's right, every two months you can harvest rich plant food, right in your backyard. You also get eggs.

This plan is a true form of recycling. People waste a tremendous amount of food every day, but the chickens living on your compost pile will be more than happy to eat your leftovers and convert them into eggs and fertilizer. Yesterday's spaghetti, a stale loaf of bread, an unfinished bowl of popcorn, you name it, the chickens will eat it. They will squawk happily when they see you coming with the leftover bowl, whatever it contains, however messy.

You may be wondering what this has to do with a stress-reducing garden. The answer is a lot. As we've already learned, social scientists are finding that one of the reasons our society is in such big trouble is that we are so detached from the natural process. Most of us are totally out of touch with the production of the food that we eat. Well, here is your opportunity to make a real, live, natural connection.

Besides, chickens are some of the funniest animals around. Each and every hen has her own personality, and if you keep two around for a while, you will make this discovery for yourself. My chicken Evodia, whom I have had since she was an egg, has more personality than many of the bureaucrats working and living in Washington, D.C. She runs around, barks at people, and provides me with a never-ending source of amusement.

Chickens can be bossy, though. If I don't have any good leftovers for Evodia and she is forced to dine on standard chicken feed, she will hoot and holler for at least ten minutes. When I get home and run out to see Evodia and collect her egg of the day, she greets me with a cackle and jumps up and down, looking for the treat I might have in hand. (Chickens are a bit mercenary, but then, who isn't?)

As I have mentioned, I live in the city, but surprisingly enough, no one has ever complained about my chickens. Of course, I have a fence around my property, so the neighbors don't have a chance to see the birds, and hens aren't very noisy. Do make certain you get hens—a rooster would definitely tip folks off to the fact that you have more than a Fido residing in your backyard! Roosters don't lay eggs, so they really are a fairly worthless commodity in our plan. Stick to the hens, and you shouldn't have a problem. And believe it or not, chickens don't smell. They only smell when you have 5,000 in a space in which 300 could live happily. If 100 people lived in a house built for four, it would smell pretty bad, too.

Chickens are easy to keep, and depending on where you live, they can stay outside all winter. You do need to provide cover for your chickens—no one likes to get rained on. Go to the library and check out a book on backyard poultry keeping, and you will find all you need to know about keeping a chicken or two.

STRESS-ERCISES

❦ *One* ❦

After dinner, collect all leftovers and feed them to your chicken friends. Make certain to talk to the birds as you do.

❦ *Two* ❦

In the morning, run out to the chicken coop and gather eggs for your morning breakfast. Go back inside and fry yourself one.

❦ *Three* ❦

Save up all your eggs for a week or two, make homemade pasta, and serve it for dinner when friends come over.

❦ *Four* ❦

Take a chair out and sit next to your chicken coop. Watch your two chickens interact. Try to notice the differences in their personalities. Get to know them personally. To warm them up to you, you might want to offer them the occasional worm. I have found that this pleases my hens to no end.

❦ *Five* ❦

Boil some spaghetti and feed it to your pets. They will think it is worms and get all excited. Did you ever see a chicken with spaghetti hanging out of its bill? This will take your mind off your troubles for at least half an hour.

• • •

I strongly suggest that you convert your compost pile into a chicken coop; you will have more fun with your feathered pets than you can even begin to imagine. Of course, you don't have to get chickens if you don't want to, but you do need to fill your garden with diversions. Be it a water garden with some fish swimming around in it or a compost pile with some chickens running around on it, a garden becomes fun when you supply it with fun items. As I said at the beginning of the book, you need to find out what will act as an amusement for you. For me, spending half an hour between the chickens and the water garden takes me out of my regular life. It offers me some time away from the all-too-familiar demands and pressures. When I go out to my garden with a trowel and uncover an earthworm and then run it over to Evodia, I leave my stress-filled world behind and enter into a different and a better world, the world of nature.

Filling your garden with distractions will insure that you go out there and stay out there long enough for Mother Nature to come down out of the sky and smack you with her de-stressing stick. It may not happen for you in precisely that way, but something will happen, I promise you, and that something will give you great pleasure and great peace of mind.

For a good time, give your chickens some pasta, and see what happens. This is what I call "free theater."